SMALL BUSINESS

ACCELERATION

SMALL BUSINESS ACCELERATION

SECOND EDITION

GET NOTICED USING FACEBOOK, LINKEDIN, EMAIL MARKETING, PUBLIC RELATIONS, AND VIDEO MARKETING

BY PAMELA WIGGLESWORTH

EXPERIENTIAL PTE LTD

© 2014 by Pamela Wigglesworth

ALL RIGHTS RESERVED. No part of this document may be reproduced or transmitted in any form whatsoever, electronic or mechanical, including photocopying, recording, or by any information storage or retrieval system without express written, dated, and signed permission from the author.

Second Edition
Published October 2014 by Experiential Pte Ltd
www.experiential.sg

ISBN 10: 1499108958
ISBN 13: 9781499108958

Book cover design by Julie Springer

DISCLAIMER AND LEGAL NOTICES:

The information presented herein represents the view of the author as of the date of publication. Because of the rate at which conditions change, the author reserves the right to alter and update her opinion based on the new conditions.

This guide is for informational purposes only. While every attempt has been made to verify the information provided in this book, neither the author nor her affiliates or partners assume any responsibility for errors, inaccuracies, or omissions. Any slights of people or organizations are unintentional.

The author shall not be held liable for any loss of profit or any other commercial damages, including but not limited to special, incidental, consequential, or other damages. The fact that an organization or website is referred to in this work as a citation and/or a potential source of information does not mean that the author endorses the information the organization or website may provide or the recommendations it may make. Further, readers should be aware that Internet websites listed in this work may have changed or disappeared after the completion of this work.

This guide is not intended for use as a source of legal or accounting advice. If advice concerning legal or related matters is needed, the services of a fully qualified professional should be sought. You should be aware of any laws that govern business transactions or other business practices in your country and state.

Any reference to any person or business whether living or dead is purely coincidental.

Dedicated to my mother Patricia who was always there for me in all my business ventures and in life. I love you and miss you dearly.

ACKNOWLEDGMENTS

As a writer, I thought my work was done when the book was handed over to the editor. That thought could not have been further from the truth. In fact, I had a way to go before I could call this book complete.

I want to thank my editor Mary Waters, who was more than editor. I learned so much from her and the book just got better as a result of her contribution. She took the time to really read the contents. She understood my "voice" and then fine-tuned it.

Mary, I thank you for your patience and your talents. I appreciate all that you have done to assist me in delivering a polished book. It was a joy to work with you.

Thanks to Julie Springer for her catchy book cover design and for making the cover design project an easy one.

Many thanks to my husband John Wigglesworth who listened to me ramble on and on about getting a book written and then for jumping in to ensure that everything looked just right before it went off to the publishers. Thank you for your love, support and partnership.

Thank you Udo Meerkerk for your marketing knowledge and your contribution to the book.

Last, but not least, thank you to my friends Kevin Cottam and Sylvia Fernandes who were my cheerleaders, motivating me to get this book completed sooner than later. I look forward to your continued support, as this is only the beginning.

TABLE OF CONTENTS

PREFACE

It's truly the best time to be an entrepreneur. I absolutely love being an entrepreneur. In fact, some people might refer to me as a serial entrepreneur because I've set up four businesses over the span of 21 years. Yet not all of my businesses have ended in a success story.

I've even lost money big time. More than I care to mention, but I will. Let's just say it was easily close to US$60K. Ouch! It's a little less painful to think about it now, but I do think about it because it is what drives me today.

Back in 1998 I had a successful women's boutique that focused on catering to the western-size female figure. Translation: a full figure gal with hips and a generous bust. In Asia, that's just about any woman from the western world. Around that time I moved my business from a small second story shop house into your typical shopping mall. Simultaneously, when I made my move, Asia was experiencing the first Asian financial crisis.

By mid-2000 an economic slowdown was upon us and people weren't shopping as much. Come February 2001, the mall had become a ghost town and we knew the business was not going to survive. Despite my wishful thinking that I could easily get out of the lease, my requests fell on deaf ears. The landlords could have cared less that we weren't making any money. Eventually they knocked off two weeks worth of rent but we were required to pay the remaining balance on the lease. That amounted to about US40,000; equal to seven months rent.

In hindsight I realized that I lacked sufficient knowledge in marketing to sustain the business. Had I known a fraction of what I know today, chances are I might have been able to ride out that slow period and save my store.

It was tough having to take that amount of money out of my husband's and my savings. At times, the tension in the house was so thick you could cut it with a knife. Fortunately, we weathered the storm and have become stronger and closer as a result.

After the store closed I allowed myself to have a two month pity party and to reflect on my experience. At the same time, I didn't want to forget about the $40,000 that was gone. That loss eventually became the fuel that ignited my passion for marketing and working with small businesses today.

I needed to know that the $40,000 loss was not in vain, to make it count for something. This was a great learning experience for me and for others, for that matter, so I made the conscious decision to "Fail Forward."

I always knew that the day would come when I would start another business. This time I was determined to be better prepared and more knowledgeable about how to market my business to increase the probability of success.

So I dug in and learned everything I could about marketing. I listened to anyone and everyone who was willing to share with me about how to create awareness for the business, how to generate traffic and leads to a business, how to brand myself, how to increase sales. My learning was conducted over coffee, in networking sessions, and through seminars and webinars. I researched day and night and was a human sponge.

With the start of my new businesses, I applied what I had learned and saw great results. Most of what I was doing was applying techniques to increase awareness, leads, and sales in my business without the benefit of a huge marketing budget. I moved from being a student and began sharing and teaching others what I knew. The word spread about my marketing workshops and bootcamps.

Soon I was being invited to conduct the workshops and bootcamps internationally.

Sharing what I learned became my way to "Fail Forward." It will always be my passion to teach other entrepreneurs how to easily and successfully market their business. My mission is to educate others so that no entrepreneur or small business ever has to experience the financial loss that I did.

So if you're reading this book, my goal is for you too to learn simple and manageable techniques that you can apply to your business today. Keep in mind that you don't have to do everything. Pick what resonates with you, start with one or two things that you can measure, and then add another tactic. Slowly but surely you will see a change in your results.

I wish you the greatest success in your business!

Pamela

> Get connected and receive tips, tactics and techniques to market your business as well as information on upcoming workshops or bootcamps in your area. Connect with me at http://bit.ly/1mWrioU. You'll also receive a free Marketing Plan infographic.

Chapter 1

Marketing with Facebook

1.1 Introduction

Facebook is a social networking site that lets users share information, post photos and videos, play games, and otherwise connect with one another through online profiles. Founded by Harvard University students Mark Zuckerberg, Eduardo Saverin, Andrew McCollum, Dustin Moskovitz and Chris Hughes, Facebook was launched in February 2004. In 2012, Facebook began publicly trading after filing one of the largest IPOs in United States history.

In October of 2013 Facebook achieved the status of having over 1.9 billion registered members. If Facebook was a country, it would be the third largest country in the world. Now if you're an entrepreneur, that number should have you quivering with excitement. If that number had no effect on you, then let me say it again. Facebook has close to 2 billion members and depending on when you're reading this, that number could be even higher. On top of the huge membership, a disproportionate number of Facebook members are educated and tech-savvy.

1.2 Setting Up a Facebook Page

Given who is likely to use Facebook, having a presence on Facebook is a must these days. It should not serve as the cornerstone of your marketing plan, but it is an important piece of it. The easiest way to build your presence on Facebook involves setting up a Facebook Company Page, hereinafter referred to as a Facebook Page.

Facebook Pages (see Fig. 1.1) are similar to personal Facebook profiles; however, they are tailored for businesses, organizations, companies, brands, entities, etc.

Previously called Fan Pages, Facebook Pages are designed to help you reach out to and interact with your fan base, your community, your tribe, as it were. Virtually any major brand, company, or celebrity has a Facebook Page, and so should you.

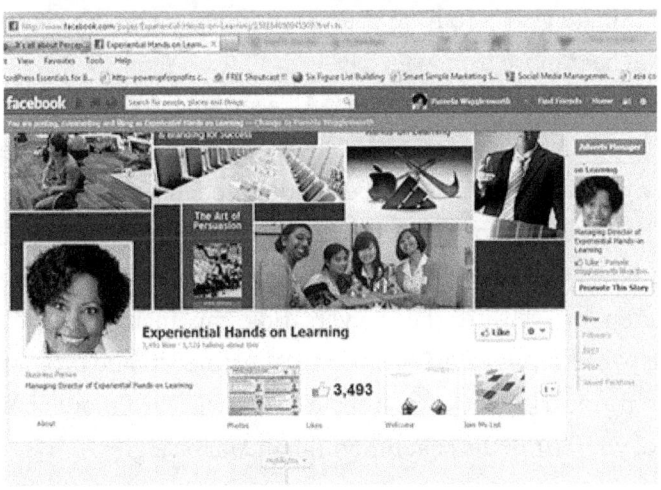

Fig. 1.1 A Facebook Page is an important component of social media marketing.

Sometimes I hear people say that Facebook is not appropriate for their industry and therefore they feel they should forego having a Facebook Page.

Given that Facebook provides you with an opportunity to share news, insights, images, videos, and more importantly, content for FREE, why wouldn't you jump on this opportunity?

> It's not costing you anything, so why wouldn't you want to reach out to prospects with this social networking platform?

Let me also add one important factor before deep diving into how to get started. As just mentioned above, Facebook is a platform that allows you to engage with your community. As a marketer, (yes, that includes you even if you go by a different title), your role is to have an ongoing conversation with your community. I view Facebook as a place to chat with people and build your credibility and trust factors. Your ultimate goal is to have your community members Like you so they can hear more from you.

Before you set up your page, I recommend that you capture names and email addresses of your Facebook friends and keep the list in a separate file. You will be posting updates on your Facebook Page, but you want to be able to keep the conversation going outside of Facebook. Once people are away from Facebook and reading your newsletter or website, the conversation can include selling your product or service. Leave Facebook for the fun stuff and promote and sell from your newsletter or website. You will learn more about the value of your list in the chapter on Email Marketing.

Setting up a Facebook Page is very easy. The person who sets up the page is the administrator. The administrator has access to certain tabs and fields that users who view the page do not. The administrator works with the "back end" of the page; the users see the "front end."

When you are logged into your account and looking at your Timeline (home page), you'll see that the option to **Create a Page** is located in the menu that runs along the left-hand side of the screen. You'll find it under the section titled "Pages." Alternatively, you can go to http://www.facebook.com/pages/create.

Once you click on **Create a Page**, you are in administrator mode. First, you will be asked to choose the type of page you want. The choices include "Local Business or Place," "Company, Organization or Institution," "Brand or Product," and so on. These categories are simply for classification purposes. There is no advantage to having one type of page over another. The steps for setting up each page differ slightly, but the information you will be filling in is pretty much the same. The directions that follow are for the "Local Business or Place" page.

First, you will be asked to fill in some basic information, including the name, address, and phone number of your company. For these fields, and for subsequent fields you can always change information you enter and you can add information later that you may not have at your fingertips.

After you have completed the basic information and clicked **Get Started**, you will be taken to the **Set Up** for your page. The **Set Up** screen is where the real work begins, but it need not be cumbersome. Most of the customizable areas are clearly marked. Information you enter in the Set Up fields will be displayed to users in the format you are accustomed to seeing when you view a Facebook Page. Fig. 1.1 is an example of a Facebook Page as seen by users.

Notice that there are four tabs on the Set Up page: About, Profile Picture, Add to Favorites, and Reach More People. In the example shown in Fig 1.2, a Facebook Page is being set up for a business called "My New Restaurant."

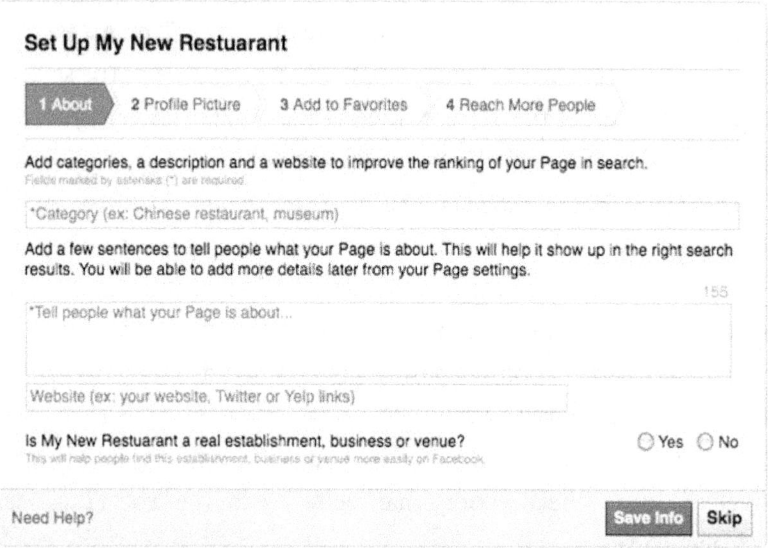

Set Up My New Restuarant

| 1 About | 2 Profile Picture | 3 Add to Favorites | 4 Reach More People |

Add categories, a description and a website to improve the ranking of your Page in search.
Fields marked by asterisks (*) are required.

*Category (ex: Chinese restaurant, museum)

Add a few sentences to tell people what your Page is about. This will help it show up in the right search results. You will be able to add more details later from your Page settings.

155

*Tell people what your Page is about...

Website (ex: your website, Twitter or Yelp links)

Is My New Restuarant a real establishment, business or venue?   ⃝ Yes ⃝ No
This will help people find this establishment, business or venue more easily on Facebook.

Need Help?   Save Info | Skip

Fig. 1.2 Set Up screen for a business titled "My New Restaurant" Notice that the About tab is selected.

With the About tab selected, you are asked to provide a category, a brief description of your brand and, optionally, a link to a website. The information you enter in these fields is very important. When users view your Facebook page (the "Front End"), they will see an About tab (see Fig 1.3). When they click on this tab, they will see the information you've entered on the Set Up screen (Basic Info and Contact Info).

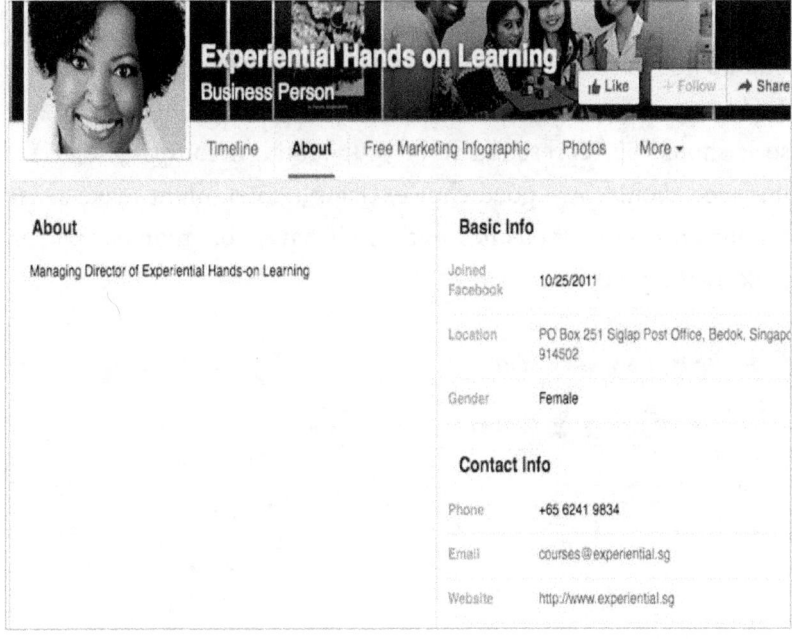

Fig.1. 3 When users click the About tab, they will see information you enter on the **Set Up** screen in the format shown here.

You want two things to happen when users click the About tab: first, if users were actively searching for your brand or company, you want them to know they have landed in the right place so that they feel comfortable Liking your content. Second, if they were not actively searching for your brand or company, you want to provide enough content for them to get a good feel for what you have to offer and why you provide value. Hopefully, this in turn will lead them to Like your page. Getting users to Like your page is the goal here, because once they have Liked it, any updates you post are more likely to appear in their news feed until they Block your page.

After you complete the information for the About tab and click Save Info, you will be taken to the Profile Picture tab (see Fig. 1.4).

At the very least, your page should contain a profile photo. Use the Add Photo tab to add an image that will be your page's profile photo. This image will be linked to any messages you send out to your fans, so it should be representative of your brand. A company logo, for instance, would be a good choice. Using a logo might make sense for entrepreneurs or businesses that will have more than one person making the posts on the site.

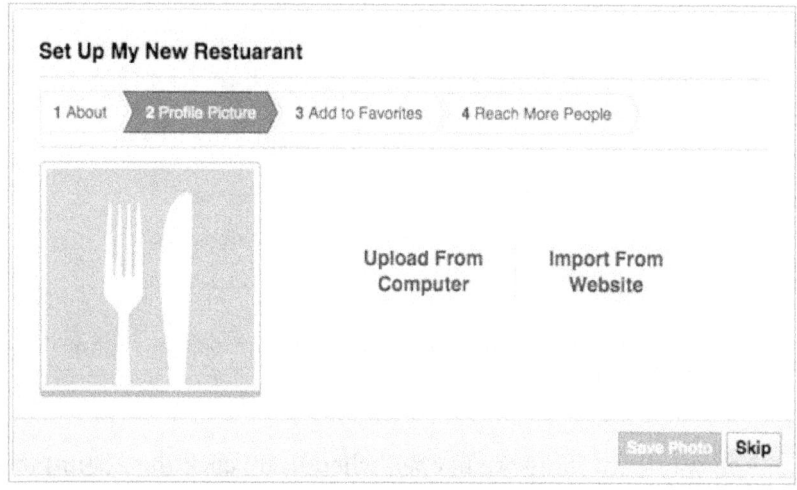

Fig. 1.4 The Profile Picture tab gives you the option of adding a photo from your computer or the Web.

Fig. 1.5 Administrator's home page, with an example of how the Profile Picture will appear once the setup is complete. Be sure to Like your page!

Fig. 1.6 An example of how the home page and Profile Picture will appear to users. Notice that a cover photo has not yet been added.

The third tab on the Set Up screen, Add to Favorites, allows you to add a link to your Company page on your Favorites (or Bookmarks) bar. The link will show up next to your other Favorites (the example shows News Feed, Messages, and Events as favorites). Simply click Add to Favorites and you're all set.

Set Up My New Restaurant

1 About   2 Profile Picture   3 Add to Favorites   4 Reach More People

FAVORITES
News Feed
Messages
Events   2

Add your Page to your favorites to easily access it anytime.

My New Restaurant

Add to Favorites

Skip

Fig. 1.7 Add to Favorites tab on the Set Up screen.

Next, you will be taken to the fourth tab, Reach More People.

Fig. 1.8 The Reach More People tab on the Set Up screen gives you the option to set up an account for paid advertising you may want to invest in.

The Reach More People tab invites you to establish a payment method so that you are ready to go when you want to take advantage of Facebook's advertising options. Clicking on **Add Payment Method** lets you set up an account using either PayPal or your credit card. If you skip this step, you can always set up an account later.

When you finish with this tab, you will be taken to the administrator's home page, where there are more options to customize your page. When you are logged into your Facebook account, you will always see your Company page from the Administrator's view. To see your page as users see it, you will need to log into Facebook with a different account.

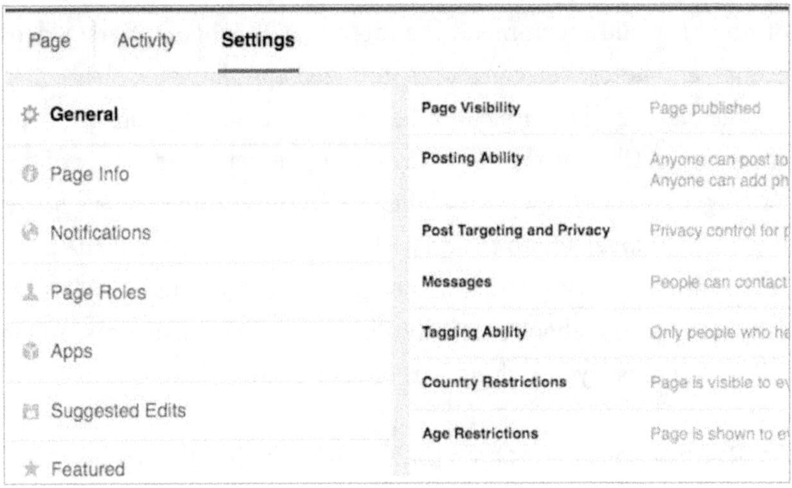

Page	Activity	**Settings**		
⚙ **General**		Page Visibility	Page published
⊕ Page Info		Posting Ability	Anyone can post to Anyone can add ph
✎ Notifications		Post Targeting and Privacy	Privacy control for p
⚖ Page Roles		Messages	People can contact
⚙ Apps		Tagging Ability	Only people who he
		Country Restrictions	Page is visible to e
▣ Suggested Edits		Age Restrictions	Page is shown to e
★ Featured			

Fig. 1.9 You reach the Settings screen (equivalent to a "control panel" by clicking on the Settings tab on the administrator's home page.

The Settings screen lets you customize your page and input additional information. The first four links on the left-hand side (General, Page Info, Notifications, Page Roles) are the most important. You should complete the fields associated with these links first. The fields for each link are self-explanatory; the Page Info section is the one you will want to spend the most time on. Here, you will be able to add information to the basic description you completed in the preliminary setup. The information you enter here will appear in the About section.

Next, go to the **Page Roles** page and input the names or emails of individuals who will have administrative access. Be sure to define their roles. It should be noted that the people you select will have to be Facebook members to accept an admin position.

When you have completed this information, go to the **Apps** page and add or update any apps you think are a good fit for your page. As of now, I would recommend the three that Facebook offers: video, events, and notes. You can add customized apps later.

The last step is to upload a horizontally aligned photo for your cover photo. Click on the Page tab in the upper left hand corner of the **Settings** screen. This will take you back to the administrator's home page. Click **Cover Photo** to add a photo. Make the most of the page real estate by creating something engaging here, as this is the largest graphic space Facebook currently allows page administrators, and it will be the most eye-catching part of your page.

1.3 Recruiting People to Like (Follow) Your Page

Once everything is in place, it is time to market your page. You have a few options when it comes to marketing your page, some of which are free. Let us take a look at both free and paid options.

When it comes to free methods of promoting your page, you can do one of two things. You can manually invite people to Like your page, which involves selecting any of the administrator's list of contacts (Facebook friends) or sending out email invitations (assuming the email you are sending the invite to is the same email that person uses for their Facebook account). Doing this is very simple, but nobody likes spam, so please be mindful of whom you invite to Like your page.

> If your page is relatively empty, inviting people too soon may turn them off and ruin your chance of ever getting them to Like the page. For this reason, I recommend filling out the page with content and updates before inviting anyone to Like it.

Fig. 1.10 Contact friends and invite them to follow your Facebook Page after you have added content and updates.

One obstacle businesses must overcome when starting a Facebook Page involves not having any followers (Likes). When you arrive on a Facebook Page that has few to no Likes, it is a sign that the business has not gained any traction online. Yet how do you get followers and avoid the trap of being Unliked (or ignored) when you are brand new? Well, you can invite your friends and family to Like your page, but that can be a slow and relatively ineffective process.

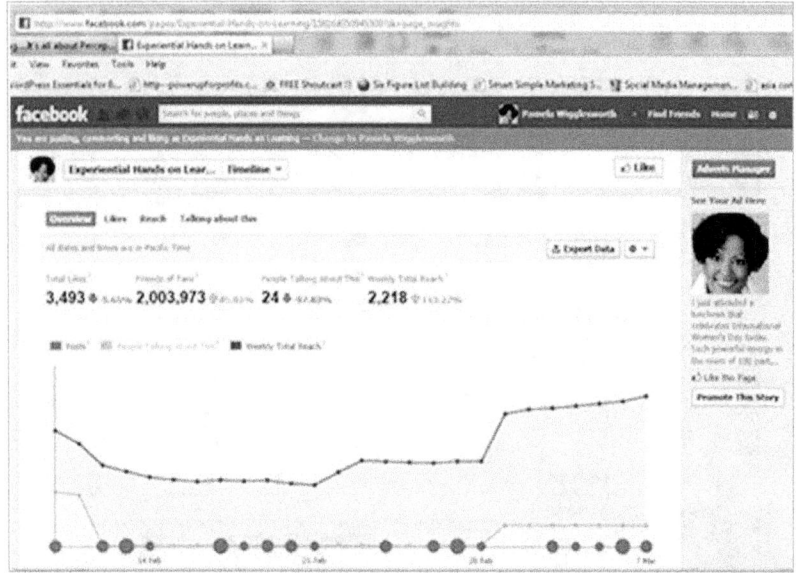

Fig. 1.11 Monitor your Likes and the number of people you reach with the Activity Log.

In the following sections, I will show you how to increase the number of followers you have, either by running a contest on Facebook or by using paid advertising, so don't get discouraged and jump to the next chapter.

1.4 RUNNING A CONTEST ON FACEBOOK

Now that your Facebook Page is complete and you have some followers in place, it is time to use your page to start promoting your business. If you only have a few Likes, I would recommend holding off on a contest until you have built up followers from your website or from paid advertising, which is explained below. With that said, running a contest on your website instead of your Facebook Page, and pointing participants to your Facebook Page, is a great way to build up the number of authentic followers very quickly.

Before I dive into contests, there are some things you should note. Facebook is very particular about how you use it to promote contests. In short, contests must be run through the proper channels. There is good reason for this requirement.

The main reason Facebook has so many regulations surrounding contests is that there are unscrupulous companies out there who desire to exploit the huge user-base and ease of access to information that comes with Facebook. Because of this, you may not promote contests through your followers' personal timelines. In other words, you can't ask participants to share anything on their profiles as part of the contest. Instead, you must run contests through your page or an application. (For a full list of guidelines please visit Facebook's **Promotion Guidelines** page). Fortunately, there are companies dedicated to providing apps that make running Facebook contests very easy. Further, running a contest with these apps can be relatively inexpensive.

Although it is beyond the scope of this publication to cover the wide array of companies that dedicate themselves to running Facebook promotion applications, some of the most popular ones are listed below.

- Strutta—Great for professional, beautiful looking campaigns, but on the costlier side ($250 - $1000 per promotion).

- WooBox—Prices range from $1 to over $1000 depending on the number of fans your page has; campaigns are easy to set up.

- Rafflecopter—Free for simple giveaways, up to $60/month for packages that include additional support and analytics.

In addition to these companies, a quick search on Google for "Facebook contest apps" will provide you with more than enough information to make an informed choice. Just remember that you need a high number of eyeballs on the contest to make it worth your while. If you only have 500 visitors a month coming to your home page, running a contest may not make sense. If you have 5,000 or 50,000, it may be a great way to get a huge number of new hits on your Facebook Page.

1.5 How to Run a Paid Advertising Campaign on Facebook

Using paid methods to build your online presence is something that should be carefully considered. If you plan to use your Facebook Page as a marketing channel, you could potentially build your fan base and the number of leads you have for pennies on the dollar. However, if you do not plan on *consistently* using your Facebook Page to send followers to your blog, website, or sales page, paying to build your online presence may not be a good way to spend your time and money.

If you decide you want to go the paid route, you can start the process by going to the Facebook advertising page (https://www.facebook.com/advertising). This will take you to Facebook's paid advertising introduction. On this page, you have the option to create an ad. If you select this option, you will be taken to the Ad Manager page. Or, you can go to the administrator home page and click on Build an Audience to reach the ad manager page.

Fig. 1.12 From the administrator home page, you can go to the Ad Manager page from the Build Audience drop-down menu.

Because setting up paid advertising is straightforward, and because Facebook offers a Help Center and User Forum, I will not be providing a step-by-step guide. Still, there are some basic pointers that can help you target the right audience and build up your following.

Fig. 1.13 Facebook advertising is another way to increase your pool of followers.

For starters, Facebook ads have clear parameters. They point to one URL (which can be your Facebook Page or an outside link), allow you to use one graphic thumbnail image, and allow one title header and two lines of descriptive text. Because the amount of text allowed is so limited, it's important to supplement your ad with a well-chosen, quality image that represents your brand.

Targeting your ad is rather simple. You can target your audience using basic demographic qualifiers such as gender, age, and location, or you can target them by their interests (including other pages they have Liked). So, if you had a candy company, targeting users who have Liked M&Ms would not be a bad idea. I suggest targeting your ads to your core demographic (such as men between the ages of 18 and 23 who live in California) versus using interest-based targeting— although both can be effective.

When it comes to bidding, make sure you note the difference between each ad's bid and the campaign's budget. The campaign budget dictates how much your entire campaign can spend per day, while the ad bid dictates how much you will spend per click or per thousand impressions. An impression, sometimes called a view or an ad view, is the one-time display of an ad on a web page, whether the ad is clicked on or not. The number of impressions is an estimate of the number of people a particular advertisement is reaching and is one way of measuring the effectiveness of the ad.

Instead of the impressions model, I would highly recommend using the per-click model as it gives you significantly more control over your ads. Further, if you start to see a very high CTR (click thru ratio) on your ads, you can always crunch the numbers to see if paying per thousand impressions would be more profitable.

From here, I would advise writing a minimum of four different ads for each page or URL you are sending traffic to. In most ad tests, the ads that perform best are the ads that marketers thought would perform worst, and vice versa. So rather than assuming you are the world's best copy writer and know what ads will best convert into sales, throw a dozen or so ads up and let the data be the judge.

Another way to advertise on Facebook is through the use of Promoted Posts. Promoted Posts are a good way to get your content in front of users who are not currently following you, as well as fans who might not be checking their newsfeed at the time you post an update. Like ads, Promoted Posts can be targeted to a specific audience. Also, as with ads, you control and set the budget. Unlike an ad, however, a Promoted Post will appear in the content feed, rather than in the sidebar.

> Before getting started with ads that include images and video, I recommend that you first go to the Facebook help page, "How to create an ad."

There are specific guidelines for how much text your ad can have (no more than 20 percent of the image). I learned this the hard way after investing in special graphics to boost the post, only to find that my images did not meet Facebook's 20 percent text rule. In this same section you can also find out what you need for uploading videos.

When it comes to the budget, Facebook will generate a suggested budget for your ad. You do not have to accept this amount. Most people don't know that they have the option to select the budget that they want. I usually start out with $5.00 per day and run an ad for seven days. Thirty-five dollars a week is a reasonable amount to pay to reach a large targeted audience.

To boost or promote a post, simply create the post on your Facebook Page as you normally would. This can be any update, news item, or photo you would ordinarily place in your page's feed. When creating your ad, ensure you include some type of call to action; for example, Click here; Register today; or Sign up now.

After your post has been created, click on the megaphone icon that appears on the top of the post, or click on the **Boost Post** link at the bottom. Doing either one of these will launch a pop-up window that allows you to choose your audience and budget settings. Clicking **More Options** at the bottom of the window will allow you to optimize additional settings for your post, including how long the post is promoted.

You can see how your post is doing by looking at the number on the bottom of the post itself. The number indicates how many people have seen the post. Clicking this number will reveal the number of followers who saw your post in their regular feed versus how many people saw it through paid promotion. If your post is not doing well, you can change your target settings or choose to boost a different post.

Aside from running contests and using paid ads and posts, I suggest that you start small and work your way up. Paid advertising can be a great source of leads, but if it is not managed properly *you can end up spending hundreds of dollars with nothing to show for it.* Given this risk, it is best to begin running a highly targeted group of ads to a highly defined demographic using a small daily budget. If this method shows promise, you can always expand your demographic and increase your daily budget.

While an entire book could be written about how to set up a Facebook Page and how to attract paid traffic to it, the above directions will get you well on your way to having an established presence on Facebook. As mentioned earlier, if you have any questions after playing around with the page and ads for a while, Facebook offers a Help Center and User Forum. Another way to seek help is to type your problem into Google.

1.6 Best Practices for Facebook

The best way to think of social networks is to imagine them as a cocktail party. People are chatting, engaging with one another, and generally having fun sharing information. In this setting, nobody likes the guy who is bouncing from person to person screaming and shouting about his product or service and trying to sell something.

I came across this analogy a long time ago and it is probably the most perfect social media marketing analogy in existence. Long story short: don't be the annoying party guy! Rather than forcing your product or service on people who are just trying to have fun while sharing information, give them something fun, informative, or both to share. Make them want to share your information. There is no form of marketing easier than word-of-mouth, and the guy with the shiny new toy (bit of information) doesn't have to promote himself during the party; instead partygoers ooh and ah and tell others on his behalf.

Fig. 1.14 Give your followers more. Post links of other people's content as well as your own.

In the next chapter we will look at how you can use LinkedIn to build leads and promote your business. LinkedIn is very similar to Facebook except that it is geared toward executives and other professionals and has a relatively smaller user base.

1.7 Take Action Exercise

1. Set up a Facebook Page. Begin establishing a Facebook presence by creating a page for your brand. Go through all the steps of populating your page, including uploading a profile and cover photo, filling out the description for the **About** section, and personalizing the settings on the **Page Info** section. Create an engaging Timeline Cover. Take some time, several days if necessary, to ensure that your page accurately reflects your brand and your brand's objectives.

2. Create a Paid Ad. Test the waters with paid advertising. Create an ad aimed at generating traffic toward your newly created Facebook Page. Target your ad to a specific demographic and their interests. Set a small test budget and monitor your ad's performance closely.

3. Create a Promoted Post. You should be posting content on your Facebook Page regularly. Choose one of these posts—ideally a relevant one—and promote it to a specific audience. Set a reasonable budget and watch your numbers to see how your post performs.

4. Post regularly to your Facebook Page with engaging content. Share other people's content as well as your own. Include images and videos as these items are the most shared content. I would suggest at least twice a week, daily if you can.

5. <u>Time management for posts.</u> If you are concerned that posting on Facebook will take up too much of your time, consider hiring a freelancer to make your social media posts or consider using a social media app such as HootSuite, Tweetdeck or Buffer App to write and schedule your posts at the times and dates of your choosing.

Chapter 2

Marketing with LinkedIn

2.1 INTRODUCTION

For those of you with B2B businesses, or who cater to professionals, LinkedIn is the place to be. As of this writing, LinkedIn had over 300 million professionals, including executives, in its network. While this is only a fraction of the membership found on Facebook, there is no network on earth with more members who are successful professionals.

Keep in mind, though, that LinkedIn is a different animal than Facebook. Within LinkedIn, spam is even more heavily frowned upon, and paid advertising is just now gaining traction. Nevertheless, any company that wants to be taken seriously these days needs to be present on LinkedIn.

Fig. 2.1 Increase your reach with LinkedIn.

2.2 How to Fully Utilize Your LinkedIn Profile

Setting up a profile on LinkedIn is similar to setting one up on Facebook, except that LinkedIn asks for significantly more information. While getting your profile 100 percent filled out will take some time, it is worth the effort, as having a professional profile could mean the difference between a powerful partner or investor reaching out to you (or not).

Along the same lines, professionals who do not have a fully filled out profile are not taken as seriously as those who do. Further, professionals who do not post a profile picture in professional-looking attire are not taken as seriously. Make sure you do both. The more time you spend building your profile, the more ways you enable others to find you and connect with you to do business.

> To fully utilize your profile, make sure that you fill out as many of the relevant sections as possible. The top of your profile, which is the first area people will see, highlights your name, title, the company you work for, your location, and what industry you are involved in. In the section that lists your title, give some thought as to what you want to list.

Write in a manner that tells others how you help versus just a job title. If there is enough space, include your website within the title section. My profile says Speaker, Trainer, Presentations Skills Coach | Marketing Communication @www.experiential.sg. There are a limited number of characters for this section so play around with what you want to say until you get it just right.

You will also have the opportunity to claim what is referred to as your vanity URL. This is your personalized LinkedIn URL. Ideally the URL should include your name (if it isn't already taken). If your name is unavailable, then come up with a clever way of creating a unique URL or consider adding your middle initial to the URL. Once you have finished creating your profile, don't forget to click the link that will make your profile public. In other words, your profile can now be found through the search engines and you definitely want that for marketing your business.

Ensure that you keep this information up-to-date, and that you use the company, location, and title that have the strongest impact and make you look as professional and powerful as possible.

In the **Summary** section of the **Profile** page, highlight your strong points as a professional while not going overboard. There is nothing worse than coming upon someone who has written a short novel in his or her summary section. Don't be that person. Instead, briefly highlight your current work, your work history, and your education (only highlight your degree if you have something above a Bachelor's degree; there will be another section for education later).

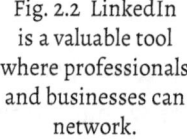 

Fig. 2.2 LinkedIn is a valuable tool where professionals and businesses can network.

The **Experience** section is where you can expand on your work history and the unique skills you possess. Once again, nobody wants to read a novel, but this is a good area for highlighting your successes and the skills you developed at your previous jobs—focusing, of course, on your strongest skill set.

From here you can fill in the **Skills and Areas of Expertise** section. List your five or so strongest areas of expertise or skills. They should be highly related to the job you are currently performing, the set of skills you are currently developing, or both. Other LinkedIn users can find you by searching for individuals with these skills, so you want to ensure that when they search, your profile stands out. Do not highlight skills you want to be strong in but are currently weak in; the users on LinkedIn are smart, and will know if you are trying to pull a fast one on them.

After you have updated your skills and expertise, you can complete the **Education** section. Unless you have an Ivy League degree or are fresh out of college, you do not need to list anything beyond what school you went to, what years you were there, and what your major was. If you have an advanced degree, you should definitely highlight it here. This is the time to expand on any major achievements or awards you obtained while working on your advanced degree (research awards, business achievements, etc.).

Next is the **Recommendations** section. Once you have a solid number of connections (people you are connected to on LinkedIn), you can begin to ask your bosses, coworkers, and clients for recommendations. Recommendations are endorsements from your peers that add social proof to your profile. While it is easy to talk all day about how great you are, getting someone else to talk about how great you are is a million times more powerful. Don't abuse your ability to request recommendations, though, and be ready to offer to provide a recommendation to the person who is giving one to you. Don't wait for them to request it.

The **Additional Information** section will highlight any websites you own, your Twitter handle (if you so desire), and any groups that you are part of. I highly recommend joining relevant groups, as professional memberships are a great way to show that you are involved in the community, which can lead to more networking opportunities.

Near the bottom of the page you will see the **Honors and Awards** section. I recommend listing only very high achievements here (as in awards, honors, and achievements people have actually heard of).

In the final section, you can list the types of activities you are interested in that people can contact you about. Examples include job offers, business deals, new ventures, getting in touch, etc. This section, along with the **Skills & Areas of Expertise** section, are the main ways in which people will find you on LinkedIn, so I recommend being totally honest when making your selections.

On a final note, the importance of being thorough and honest when filling out your profile can't be stressed enough. Intelligent professionals and executives can spot a fraudulent profile when they see one, so don't waste anybody's time. Bear in mind, the more thorough you are when filling out your profile, the more likely it is that people will be impressed when they land on it (and as a result, contact you).

2.3 How to Create a Company LinkedIn Page

Creating a page for your company is very simple, and is similar to creating a personal profile. If you do not already have a Company Page, simply log into your account and click on **Companies** under the

Interests tab in the top navigation bar.

It might be worthwhile to see if anyone else has already set up a company with the same name as yours—or if there are fraudsters acting as if they are the owners of your business. Assuming you do not get any results from this check, scroll down and click on **Create a Company**. After you go through the email verification, which requires that you have an email at your website's domain (meaning that your Yahoo! and Gmail email addresses do not count), verify the email they send you.

Once you have confirmed your email, you can begin to fill out your company's profile. It is worth noting that your company's profile will be shorter than your personal profile, and should not take very long to fill out. The only other important section you will want to fill out is the **Products & Services** page, which highlights the products and services you offer.

Now that your page is set up, you can promote it to the world. As with Facebook, there are a variety of ways you can promote your page (some are free, some require a fee). The next section will highlight how you can use LinkedIn to market your business.

Fig. 2.3 Think of LinkedIn as your online business card.

2.4 How to Market Your Business Using LinkedIn

There are a few ways that you can market yourself and your business within LinkedIn. One of the easiest ways to create awareness and recognition is to start a discussion. But before you start any discussions, you will need to join some relevant LinkedIn groups.

Think about groups where you can make a contribution. When I say make a contribution, this is about you first acknowledging other peoples' posts (discussions) by Liking them and sharing your own views about what you read.

Listen in (read, that is) on the conversations and then begin to make comments. After some time, begin to start your own discussions. Start by making a statement, sharing another person's article or blog post, add your thoughts and then ask a question that will get people talking.

Another way to start a discussion is to take the first few sentences from an article or blog post you wrote and then ask a question. Leave a bit.ly link that takes people to the full article or blog on your website. Instead of leaving a typical letters and numbers bit.ly link, make it engaging by customizing the link. For example, if your blog post is about Facebook advertising, then you want to capture the reader's attention even more strongly with an engaging link like http://bit.ly/marketwithFacebook. The customized short link entices the reader to read more.

As with Facebook, you can promote your LinkedIn Company Page in a variety of ways. Just as I recommended that you stay away from using family and friends to get Likes for your Facebook Page, suggesting your Company Page to employees, coworkers, colleagues, clients, etc., will probably be more successful than getting Likes from family and friends. Given that professionals you do business with are already engaged with your organization, they are less likely to view the suggestion as spam. Be careful to suggest your page only to people you know, though, as spamming on LinkedIn is highly frowned upon, and can get you in trouble faster than it will on Facebook.

Your Company Page is not the only tool you have on LinkedIn. If you are looking to build high-level relationships, connecting with other members using your profile is your best bet. You have to be careful here, though. High-level executives and power players are contacted all the time by various individuals looking for handouts and they can't afford to waste time. So before you contact them asking for something, try and build a real relationship with them.

> Provide value, send relevant blog posts that could help these executives advance their business, and do anything you can to avoid getting categorized as someone looking for a handout.

Implementing this tactic effectively is beyond the scope of this book, but it is one of the most powerful skills you can learn. If you can learn how to provide value to others without seeking something in return, an endless number of doors will open and opportunities will abound.

2.5 How to Use LinkedIn Paid Advertising

The last method you can use to promote your business on LinkedIn involves paid advertising. Paid advertising on LinkedIn is different from advertising on Facebook in a variety of ways. To begin with, you can target users on LinkedIn with more accuracy than you can on Facebook. Aside from being able to target users by gender, age, and location, you can also target them based on their job title, the school they went to, the company they work for, their skills, and the groups they belong to. And because people on LinkedIn are more selective with the groups and companies they associate with, these categories are likely to be more accurate than those on Facebook.

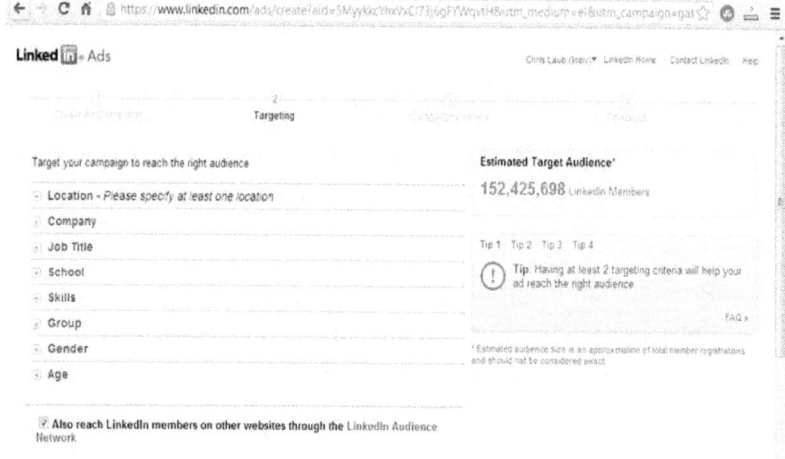

Fig. 2.4 LinkedIn offers targeting that is more fine-tuned than Facebook's targeting.

At the bottom of the advertising page, LinkedIn will give you an option to advertise to members when they are on websites other than LinkedIn (tracking is done based on cookies). This feature is similar to Google's content network, and should be used only by members who know what they are doing. When you get to know this feature, you'll see that it's an easy way to get more impressions than if you limit yourself to ads that appear only on LinkedIn.

The last thing to take note of is that LinkedIn requires a minimum budget of $10/day while Facebook does not. Once again, paid advertising can be a great way to generate leads and spread the word about your business, but should only be used by those who know what they are doing. And if you do not know what you are doing, start small until you have a better understanding of how paid advertising works. There is always time to scale up the campaign and spend more.

In addition to ads, LinkedIn also offers Sponsored Updates. Like Promoted Posts offered by Facebook, LinkedIn's Sponsored Updates appear within member newsfeeds and are marked "sponsored." These types of updates are targeted and personalized, allowing you to reach users that might not otherwise be aware of your brand. As with ads, you are free to set your own budget and whether you want to be charged per click or per impression.

> LinkedIn can also be used to send messages directly to members with whom you are not connected.

The receiving audience can be specified according to characteristics similar to those used to target ads and updates. There are some limits to this platform. LinkedIn users have the ability to opt out of receiving Sponsored InMails, putting them beyond your message's reach. Additionally, guidelines are in place to ensure that members only receive an average of one Sponsored InMail every 60 days.

Perhaps most prohibitive, however, is the cost of InMail campaigns. Each InMail credit (the equivalent of messaging one person) costs $10. If you are a basic LinkedIn user with a free account, you may purchase a total of 10 credits. Business, Business Plus, and Executive Members are allotted slightly more. Still, you are severely limited as to how many individuals you can reach.

Messaging costs and limits don't apply to users with whom you are connected directly. First degree connections can be contacted through LinkedIn's messaging system for free. Alternatively, your contacts' information can be exported to a database, allowing you to use your own email for messaging. To do this, click the Connections link from your home page and select Add Connections. You will be taken to a page where you have the option to add connections from your email provider.

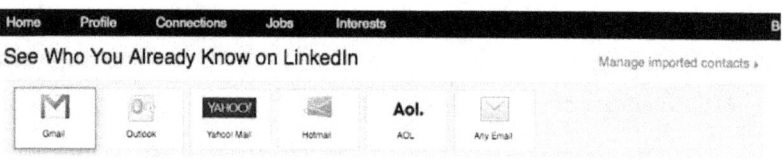

Fig. 2.5 LinkedIn will import your contacts from a variety of email providers.

Once you are on the **Connections** page, click on the **Settings** button in the top right hand corner (sprocket wheel next to the head with a plus sign). Under **Advanced Settings** on the right hand side of the screen there will be an option to **Export LinkedIn Connections.** Information can be exported to a .CSV file or a .VCF file.

2.6 BEST PRACTICES FOR LINKEDIN

The best practices I recommend for LinkedIn are similar to those I recommend for Facebook, but they are stricter. People who blatantly spam on LinkedIn, and attempt to connect with anybody regardless of affiliation, are either ignored or immediately marked as spammers by legitimate users. Don't even waste your time trying to spam people on LinkedIn. Instead, focus on how you can provide value to others, and get in the habit of offering useful information without expecting anything in return.

While paid advertising is pretty straightforward, the business of human interaction is much more complicated. LinkedIn is the largest network of professionals in the world, and the possibilities for you and your business here are endless. If you make the effort and take the time to learn how to create meaningful relationships, you can create an endless number of professional relationships and opportunities for your business.

On the other hand, if people can sense that you are just looking to benefit yourself and have nothing to offer, they will ignore you—and if you are too blatant, they will mark your messages as spam and get you blacklisted from the network. Avoid spamming at all cost. It's not worth the risk just to gain some new connections. It is best to create meaningful relationships and the rest will follow.

2.7 TAKE ACTION EXERCISE

1. Fill out your LinkedIn Profile in full so that it is 100% complete. Take some time to think about your title description. Write it in a way that tells viewers how your business can help them. Include your website if possible.

2. Research the different types of LinkedIn groups that are relevant to your business. Identify which groups are likely to have members within your target market. Join at least 10 relevant LinkedIn groups. Start commenting, liking, and sharing other members posts.

3. Start your own discussions within the groups that you have joined. Be a thought leader; share your views. Be unique and at times controversial. When people make comments to your post, be sure to acknowledge them.

4. <u>Create a LinkedIn Company Page.</u> Set up a Company Page and populate all the relevant fields with information about your brand. Pay special attention to the Products & Services section, as this is where users will learn what your company or brand offers.

5. <u>Download LinkedIn Contact Information.</u> Download your connections information to a file so that you can reach your contacts outside the bounds of LinkedIn messaging. This file is a valuable asset and should be updated regularly, as your connections grow.

Chapter 3

Email Marketing

3.1 INTRODUCTION

It's inevitable that as a business owner today you will have an email account, perhaps maybe two of three. It's become the main way we communicate with one another, even with our close friends and family. It's how we stay in touch. Think about it. When was the last time that you actually picked up the phone to have a conversation with an old friend? Even now, I rarely call my family on the phone—we Skype instead.

> In this chapter, I want to impress upon you the importance of email marketing as one of the top "must do" strategies for marketing your business. I refer to this strategy as "Keeping the Conversation Going."

In an eBook put out by HubSpot, the authors state that approximately 5 to 25 percent of the people who visit your website are ready to make a purchase. The balance is individuals who are simply doing research. Think about that for a moment. Seventy-five to ninety-five percent of the people who come to your website are just having a look around. There is no way for you to stay in contact with them unless you capture their names and email addresses. At the very least you should capture their email addresses.

As a marketer, one thing you should strive to do every day is to build your list of prospects so that you can speak to your potential customers on a regular basis, and build relationships with them. Although most of the individuals who visit your site may not be ready to buy immediately, they might be ready later on down the road. We simply don't know where people are in the buying cycle, so regular contact with them keeps you "top of mind."

When you stay in touch and educate prospects with news and information that solves their problems or answers their questions and addresses their greatest challenges, you are building rapport. Remember, people do business with people they know, like and trust. The emails you send out are ultimately building trust with your target audience.

> It's not enough just to set up an email marketing campaign; you need to ensure that you are giving your subscribers value in each email or newsletter. That means providing them with quality, high-value content.

Engage your readers by adding interesting images, static banners, audio clips. or video.

Email is particularly effective in maintaining existing relationships. Adding video to the email channel markedly increases email's power, influence and attraction. I'm all for adding anything that will increase my open rates (the percentage of people who open an email). With engaging images, video, and a strong headline, the chances of your email being opened goes up significantly Consider these statistics:

- Within 48 hours, video emails inspire a response 80 percent of the time (according to Jupiter Research).

- Video email marketing offers a return 280% higher than traditional direct mail (Gartner Research).

- People love watching video so much, we average about 32 videos a month.

When it comes to video, it can be video you create that tells about you and your company, or it can be stock footage video.

The images and stock video footage can be found from a variety of stock photography sites. Once you are ready to add images or stock footage (short video clips), look for royalty free stock photography. Royalty free refers to a type of license that gives you permission to use a stock image in certain ways. It means you are not required to pay a royalty each time you use an image. Once you've purchased a photo you can use the image in several projects without having to purchase any additional licenses.

You can find quality images for anywhere from US$1 to $20, even up to $100 depending on the source. For images that are being used for your newsletter, blog, or on a Facebook post, pricing of one to two dollars is more than reasonable. For digital purposes you only need an image that is 72dpi. I use a variety of sources: 123rf.com, Shutterstock.com, and Dreamstime.com. The first and last two sites offer free images as well, but you'll need to set up an account by registering your name and email address. When you have an account, the company watermark over the image will not show when you download an image. Be aware that free images tend to be on the site for a limited time (sometimes for only five days, with a countdown that shows when the image will be deleted). So if you see something you like at the very start of the free section, grab it and put it in your images folder.

Now let me share with you one of my favorite places to get stock footage and audio clips for free—that is, free for one week, but you are able to download 20 clips and audio mp3 files per day for seven days. Check out Video Blocks and Audio Blocks. (It's the same company for both video and audio.) You will need to give them a credit card to get started. Remember that the free session is just for one week, so if you don't want to be billed, I suggest that you put a notification in your diary to cancel your subscription before the week is out, otherwise you will be billed monthly. The annual subscription at the time of this writing is $99.00. With a subscription, you get unlimited downloads and royalty free stock footage.

In the last chapter of the book, I will be covering ways to create your own engaging video.

3.2 The Importance of Building an Email List

Most people who have been around marketing for long enough have most likely heard the phrase, "The money is in the list." To some, the idea of lists may bring to mind cold-calling and spam, but in fact there are different kinds of lists, some of which are incredibly valuable.

The lists that I am talking about are lists that you build. They are comprised of people who have *opted-in to receive content from you.* In other words, email lists are lists of people who have given you permission to market to them. Where else in the world can you get qualified leads who explicitly give you permission to contact them with valuable information and also try to sell them something, occasionally? Okay, email isn't the only place, but you get the point here. Email lists are invaluable because they are made up of people almost waving a sign saying "Hey, share some great content with me or sell me something, please!"

Keep in mind that there is a difference between buying a list of email addresses from a prospecting company and building an email list yourself. When you buy a list of email addresses and send to everyone on the list, you are simply spamming. The recipients have no idea of who you are, and no matter how qualified and targeted the list, they are highly unlikely to open your email.

I experienced this first-hand when I purchased a list of human resources managers and senior managers. Some reported me as spamming and my email service provider temporarily suspended my account until I went through a review process with them. The only way to reactivate the account was to delete this list of 400+individuals.

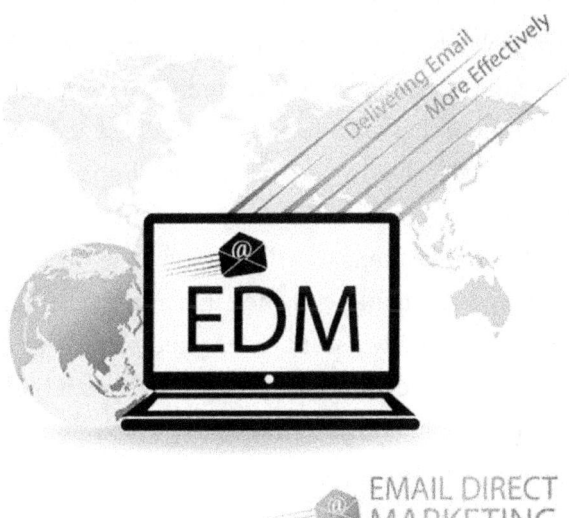

Fig. 3.1 Email marketing is a low-cost, effective means to reach your customers in a timely manner.

> Alternatively, when you build an email list of current and prospective customers who *opt in to receive content from you*, you gain full permission to market to them as you see fit.

Top-level marketers know this. Some of the top players in the online marketing industry set open rates above 91 percent. Can you imagine that? Imagine if you could get 91 percent of people you cold-called to listen to your pitch. Imagine if you could get 91 percent of people who saw your TV ad to type in your web address and visit your site. Never in a million years would this be possible.

Sadly, entry-level online marketers are scared of email marketing. They hear horror stories about how only one in 10,000 people open emails from marketers and they decide that email is unlikely to result in a positive Return on Investment (ROI). What they don't realize is that they are probably subscribed to multiple newsletters themselves, and fail to see the difference between sending out spam and sending out valuable content that includes a sales offer here and there. Reread the previous sentence. Notice that it says, "sending valuable content" and "a sales offer every now and then."

In the following sections, I will touch on the benefits of email marketing, why you should consider using a professional service provider, and more. You will want to read and reread this chapter, as a properly implemented email campaign could mean the difference between sluggish and explosive growth.

3.3 The Advantages of Email Marketing

Aside from the fact that people who sign up for newsletters are essentially giving you permission to market to them, there are a wide variety of benefits in using email as a marketing tool. For starters, the first benefit lies in the fact that digital sales channels are faster than non-digital channels.

There are three options for contacting your target audience directly. You can send them something in the mail, you can call them, or you can contact them digitally. If you have ever run a direct mail campaign via snail mail, you know how daunting it can be. First you need to design a flyer or brochure, and then pay lots of money to have it printed, print thousands of envelopes, stuff them, pay to mail them, wait while they are in the postal system, and hope they don't get thrown out when they are received. I'm not even going to touch on cold-calling campaigns (scripting, hiring full-time sales people or call centers, excessive rejection, etc.). You get the picture.

The beauty of email marketing is that none of the above scenarios is an issue. Once you have a good template designed, all you have to do is fill it in with content your target audience will find valuable. In many cases, the content doesn't even have to be yours. Some email marketers fill their newsletters with links to other sites and blogs. This sends a powerful message: "It's not all about me, and I want to do whatever I can to provide value to you." In addition, using other people's content means it takes the pressure off of you when you're experiencing writer's block or you're very busy at the time the newsletter is due to go out.

Given how easy it is to send out a campaign, there's no need to worry about not pushing hard enough. If readers find your newsletter valuable and open it 90 percent of the time, the sales pitch you send every one-in-ten emails is going to get opened. Period.

Fig. 3. 2 Great newsletter content can go viral rapidly when emails are shared.

The second benefit of using email as a marketing tool is that it is immediate. Want to talk about earth-shattering news in your industry? It could be history by the time you send the news via snail mail. With email you literally can address topics as they arise. Taking advantage of the opportunity for instant communication can position you as an authority figure and show you're on top of what's happening.

The third advantage of using email is that it allows you to focus on the specific needs of your market. Let's say that 15 percent of your market likes product A, 20 percent likes product B, 10 percent likes product C, and 55 percent likes product D. The email provider allows you to craft four different sales letters (remember your template is already done), and a few extra clicks gets you four separate, highly targeted email campaigns going out to exactly the right individuals. Targeted emailing can be done in a fast, efficient, and cost effective manner. Imagine setting up four different snail mail campaigns to target these users. The printing and mailing costs, along with the logistical requirements, would send costs through the roof. With an email campaign you don't incur any of these costs.

The fourth benefit of using email is its flexibility. Are you in an industry where connecting with your readers on a daily or weekly basis is appropriate? Imagine how much it would cost to send out a snail mail campaign every week (or day!). With email, you simply fill out your template, designate the message recipients, and voilà, you're done.

The fifth benefit of using email revolves around testing and analytics. It wasn't all that long ago that email marketers were shooting in the dark. They sent out messages and had to track their success rates with services like Bit.ly, which show how many times a URL is clicked. These days, email analytics are just as comprehensive as website analytics.

Not sure if that was a good headline to use for your newsletter? Not sure if a two-paragraph format results in longer reading times relative to a three-paragraph format? Test it. With tracking abilities that kick in when you simply copy and paste a few lines of coding into your email template, you can test every aspect of your campaign so that you can achieve maximum open rates, reading times, and click-through rates (CTRs). Combine this easy access to data with the fact that you can send out emails relatively often, and the amount of time it takes to achieve maximum effectiveness becomes very short.

Fig. 3.3 Unlike snail mail, email newsletters are delivered instantaneously.

The next benefit of using email is the ease with which email can be shared. Remember the time Bob from the office next door brought over that really awesome piece of marketing material he received in the mail? No, of course you don't, because people don't share their mail (maybe that's because interesting pieces rarely come through the mail anymore). We've all shared engaging emails with friends and family, though. Just remember: word-of-mouth marketing (in this case getting other people to send your email for you) is the easiest, cheapest, and most effective form of marketing on the planet.

The ability to track data is another benefit of email marketing. I will be going into detail about how to track data in the next, section, "Benefits of Using a Service Provider."

And last but not least, email campaigns are green. Assuming you're good about not printing things, you could build an entire campaign and send your first email blast without ever hurting a single tree. And everybody likes a green company!

In the following section I will address the benefits of using a professional service provider for your email campaigns.

3.4 THE BENEFITS OF USING SERVICE PROVIDERS

In addition to being fearful of highly ineffective campaigns, many business owners do not like email marketing campaigns because of the massive amounts of data involved. This is a legitimate concern; however it is not one that should stop you from running a campaign.

It is true that, managing the massive amounts of data that come with running an email campaign is no easy task. The good news is that there are numerous professional companies that will do this for you at inexpensive rates. With many companies like Mail Chimp offering free campaign management for lists under one or two thousand subscribers and rates around $19–$250/month to manage 50,000 subscribers, hiring a service provider is a no-brainer. Fifty thousand envelopes alone would cost $250, and that doesn't include printing brochures, postage, etc..

Aside from the low fees (the low cost of email is starting to look attractive isn't it?), there are many other benefits to using a service provider. The first benefit lies in having one database where all of your contacts are stored. If you are doing lead capture in any way, shape, or form (and you should be), using a service provider makes the entire process easy, from A to Z.

Not only do most service providers offer lead capture forms (also referred to as opt-in forms) that you can customize and have up and running in a matter of minutes, they will take the leads you get and transfer them to a simple-to-understand list in real time. Gone are the days of copying and pasting from an Excel spreadsheet into your Customer Relationship Management (CRM) software.

In most situations, your email provider will provide a wide variety of templates that you can use to send your newsletter to new and existing followers. Constant Contact, iContact and Vertical Response are just some of the more popular companies that offer this service. And if you need to customize things a little, most providers' tools are highly flexible and can be customized using HTML. Simply name your campaign, name your list, set up a lead capture form, and start sending traffic (see Fig. 3.4). It is that easy.

If, like me, you are not a technical person, simply listen to the tutorials and you're in business.

Fig. 3.4 The email service provider Mail Chimp is easy to set up and offers a free service if you have fewer than 2,000 subscribers.

Another program that is a bit more robust than the others is Infusionsoft. It too offers an email marketing service and a CRM service, but more importantly, it offers behaviour-based marketing automation.

> One of the key features of Infusionsoft is that it is behaviour-based email marketing.

Let me explain what I mean by behaviour-based. With most email programs, you prepare the email to be sent out with your links included and then schedule it to go out on the date and time of your choice. Once the email goes out you can later check the open-rates, click-throughs, and bounce rates.

Infusionsoft takes it a step further. Let's say that in your email you offered the reader a link to a downloadable free gift. Infusionsoft is tracking both those individuals who downloaded as well as those who didn't. It's watching the behaviour of the reader. If the reader doesn't download in say three days time, the system knows this and will automatically send another personalized, new message to them. "Hey Susie, how are you? I noticed you didn't download your free gift the other day. I don't want you to miss out, so here's the link again."

You can set up your email campaign so that readers are taken through a sequence depending on the actions they take. The readers then can get the sense that you are really looking out for them. Although this feature is completely automated, I've had readers write back to me to say thanks for reminding them or acknowledging that they finally downloaded a book, infographic or whatever the freebie happened to be at the time.

There is one misconception about Infusionsoft that I want to dispel for you. There is a belief among many small companies that Infusionsoft is only for companies that have 10 or more employees. This is simply not true. I know many entrepreneurs that are using this system.

Yes, it's going to take you a lot longer to fully understand and navigate the system to be up to speed, however you do get three hours of training with a Consultant.

If it seems that I'm giving this system a lot of air time, you're right. I've used iContact and Constant Contact before and I'm currently using Infusionsoft. My purpose in teaching marketing and sharing tactics, tools, and techniques is to help you shorten your learning curve and accelerate your business results. Having used the system for almost a year now and having seen all that it can do to automate my business; I honestly wish I had jumped in a lot earlier. Amongst all of its other charms, like a good back office, it automatically keeps the conversation going after I have generated my leads.

Last but not least, there is tracking. All of the big service providers, like MailChimp, AWeber, Infusionsoft and Constant Contact provide tracking as part of their campaigns. They track everything, short of what color clothes your recipients are wearing when they read (or delete) your email. No joke here. Each email service provider is set up to track how many emails were sent, when they were sent, how many unique opens you had, how many people forwarded your email, how many clicks you had (including clicks on links), how many bounces there were, and how many people opted out. This tracking information is extremely important in determining what your readers like and don't like. It should be reviewed on a regular basis.

> Make it a regular practice of adding links within the body of your newsletter. The objective here is to get your prospects in the habit of clicking on links so that when you do make an offer, they are used to clicking on a link.

It's this information that you'll want to track.

Another advantage of email service providers is that all of your newsletters can be prepared well in advance and scheduled to send at the time and date of your choice. If you know you're going on vacation for two weeks, you can easily prepare your newsletter to go out as scheduled even when you are out of the office. Don't you just love technology!

Now that we've established the importance of you building a list, I will now share with you how you can build a list using an opt-in form or an opt-in pop-up.

3.5 How to Build a List Using an Opt-In Form or Opt-In Pop-Up

While the ease and low cost of email marketing may have you excited, you are not going to find success with email if you don't have anybody to send your newsletter to. Fortunately, if you provide good content on your website, you won't have a problem building an email list.

When it comes to providing opt-in forms and opt-in pop-ups that invite a prospect to give you their email, you have two options. If your website is being run on WordPress, you can install and test different plug-ins until you find the one that best suits your site. Most opt-in forms and opt-in pop-ups can be placed using short-code slugs. For example, inserting [email_capture_form1] into the HTML of a certain page would result in the pop-up showing per the settings you have configured in the WordPress panel. If you don't want to install your own plug-ins, your service provider can offer plug-ins that will directly tie your lead capture forms to your campaign without any custom coding. This is yet another reason I highly recommend using service providers.

As for opt-in pop-ups, you have a wide variety of options if you are using WordPress. To get an idea of how many plug-ins there are that serve pop-ups, log into your WordPress dashboard, go to **Plug-ins**, and then **Add New**. In the search bar, enter "newsletter pop-up." You will see a list of different pop-up applications that insert a window in the center of a user's screen after he or she has been on your site for a defined amount of time. While some users will find this annoying, they will have been on your site long enough that they are unlikely to leave just because they had to close one tiny window. On the flip side, if your content is engaging, they most likely will sign up on the spot.

I had a pop-up opt-in form on my site for a while and then removed it when I changed email service providers. Then one day it occurred to me that I wasn't receiving as many notifications of opt-ins. The penny dropped and I realized that people were actually filling out the forms, despite the fact that the pop-up forms were somewhat annoying

I might add that many of these opt-in programs can be set so that the form pops up only when the visitor is leaving your site, or only after a person has been on the site for at least 5 seconds.

If you are not using WordPress, you are not entirely out of luck. Many of the services I have touched on offer custom contact forms that you can use on any domain you own.

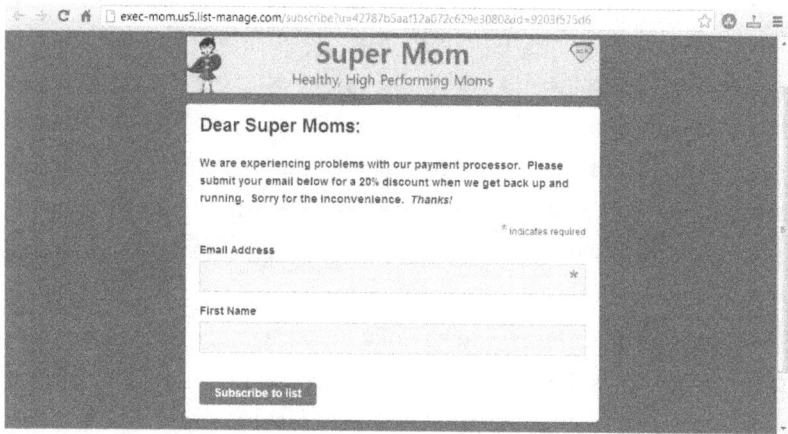

Fig. 3.5 Keep it simple. Design an opt-in form that requires just a name and email address.

Avoid the pitfall of asking for too much information from subscribers in your opt-in form. Less is more. At the onset first name and email is enough. In fact, some top marketers advocate that you should only ask for an email address. Later on when people are ready to accept an offer and want to make a purchase, that's where you'll capture more of their details.

The message in the call to action button is also important. Stay away from the word SUBMIT! No one likes to submit, so get creative with your call to action. In the example in Fig. 3.5 you can see it's as simple as 'Subscribe to list'. I've seen fun ones like, "Heck Yeah I want in'\" or '\"Count me in." You just need to get the readers to give their details and click.

Whether or not you are on WordPress, once your contact form is in place, you need to start driving traffic to it. If you are using a pop-up, virtually all incoming traffic will receive the invitation to join your newsletter. If you are using a contact form, however, you will need to drive readers to the sign-up page. There are multiple ways to do this.

For starters, sites built on WordPress can incorporate sign-up widgets into their sidebars. Many service providers offer basic plug-ins that allow site visitors to sign up for your newsletter (and have their information inserted directly into your database) right from your blog or site's sidebar (see Fig. 3.6).

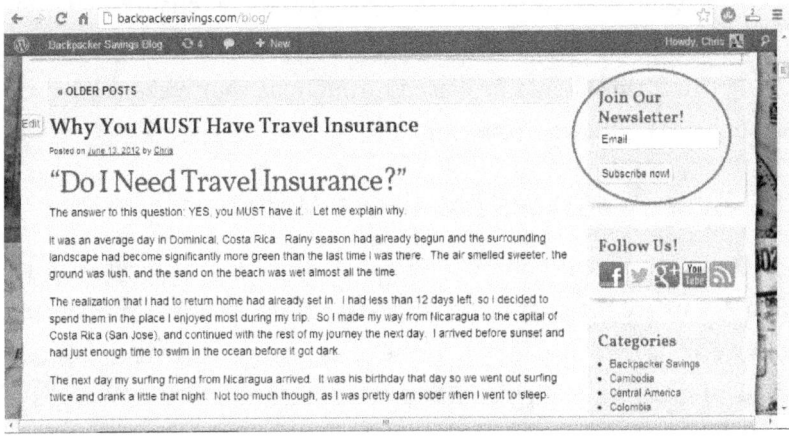

Fig. 3.6 Place an email opt-in form on your website, blog, or newsletter.

Sites that are built on WordPress can also take advantage of newsletter plug-ins that allow site owners to place miniature sign-up forms at the end of blog posts. Some can be set to display automatically at the end of every post, while some require that you place a short-code designating where you want the form to appear. Either way, what better time to get a user to sign up for your newsletter than immediately upon finishing a great piece of content?

If you are using a sign-up form on a unique URL, such as a template form provided by your service provider, you will need to send traffic directly to that URL. There are different ways to do this. For starters, you can use links with texts like "Click here to join our newsletter," or, after talking about your newsletter, you can simply use "Join now." Either way, you need to make it clear that the user needs to click on that link to get signed up. Never assume people know what they are doing; always tell them.

One thing to take into account when it comes to including an opt-in form on your website is the placement. More and more people search the Internet via their mobile devices so you want to make it easy for people to opt-in. Therefore, you want to ensure that your opt-in form is above the fold on your home page.

Opt in forms should be placed throughout your website and you should also include one on your blog.

3.6 Best Practices for Email Marketing

Odds are that if you own an email address, you receive spam. Some of us are better at protecting ourselves from spam than others, but we all have to deal with it. None of us likes getting spam, so steer clear of creating it. Remember that sending emails to prospects is based on permission marketing. The laws around the world regarding

SPAM are getting stricter every day, along with tougher penalties for individuals or companies found guilty of spamming.

The email service provider may require only that you request people to opt-in once. Today, as a suggested best practice, I recommend you implement a double opt-in for any newsletters or other program where you are gathering people's email information. This way, should someone who has opted into your list later reports you as spamming, you have a record of where they double opted-in.

However, spam is not your only concern when running an email campaign. One of the biggest mistakes you can make is with timing—emailing your subscribers too often or not often enough. If you write too often, people will quickly unsubscribe because you are bombarding them constantly with low-quality information that does not provide value. If you don't write often enough, your recipients will be surprised to see your name pop up in their inbox. If they do take the time to read your email and it doesn't impress them, they may unsubscribe so they don't have to deal with emails that add no value to their lives or to their businesses.

To find the perfect balance between writing too often and not often enough, put yourself in your subscribers' shoes. Is the industry you are in so engaging and ever-changing that it requires daily updates? Unless your site is related somehow to dispensing knowledge about an ever-changing subject (such as the subjects we find in the news), odds are you don't need to be writing your subscribers every day.

On the flip side, writing your community once a month may not be enough. If every day you are in contact with new people and are learning new lessons that may apply to your audience, take the best of the best and send out the information in a weekly update. I send out a newsletter every other week on the same day of the week and at the same time. Maintain a regular schedule so that your community will look forward to hearing from you.

Fig. 3.7 Don't spam. Invite people to opt-in to your newsletter with an opt-in box.

As for subscribers, I can't emphasize enough the importance of building an email list through opt-ins versus sending blasts to random individuals, many of whom do not desire to receive your emails. Take the time to build your email list organically, make sure you produce great content that provides value to your readers, track every aspect of your campaign, and you will have a profitable email list in no time. And while this may sound easy, it does take time.

It doesn't matter how effective your campaign is if you only have 50 subscribers. Similarly, it's irrelevant how many subscribers you have if no one opens your emails. Every aspect of email marketing requires continuous growth and a drive for perfection, but with a little bit of smart thinking, testing, and tracking, setting up a profitable email campaign is something every online marketer can (and should) do.

In the next chapter, I will talk about public relations and how you can use one of the oldest methods in the world to generate awareness surrounding your brand, product, or service.

3.7 TAKE ACTION EXERCISE

1. Give readers an opportunity to opt in. Create an opt-in form or opt-in pop-up for your page. Make sure to keep it simple. A name and an email address are sufficient.

2. Do your homework. Research email service providers to find the one that best suits your needs and your budget. Make sure to take things like customer support, tracking options, and program tutorials into consideration.

3. Design a template. Create your first newsletter or e-brochure. Take as much time as you need to make sure content is not just aesthetically pleasing, but also relevant and engaging.

4. Test the waters. Once you've ensured that tracking options are set, send your first email to either a subsection of subscribers, or to a few close associates and friends to check out first. .

5. Assess and regroup. Track your email's results. Take note of how many subscribers in your community opened your email and how many didn't. Study what links within your email were clicked on. Incorporate all of the available information into future efforts as you move forward.

6. Sign up with a royalty stock photography service. Start generating a library of images and stock footage for future use. This will save you time searching for the ideal picture when you are really pressed for time. Don't forget to check out the free images as well.

Chapter 4

Public Relations

4.1 INTRODUCTION

Since the invention of the modern printing press, companies the world over have attempted to get free coverage for their products and services. As time progressed, an entire industry was developed around the concept of getting free media coverage: the PR industry. And despite the awards and million-dollar paychecks that surround the top echelons of the industry, getting free press for your product may not be as hard as you think.

Public Relations (PR) is the process of communicating with publics, or groups of people that matter to your company in order to gain awareness and favor in their eyes. It is used to build relationships with employees, customers, partners, shareholders, potential investors, media, special interest or lobby groups, government agencies, and also the general public.

> Public relations provides a service for the company by helping to give the public and the media a better understanding of how a company works. The objective of public relations is to show the company (your business) in a positive light no matter what.

Let's be clear about this. Public Relations is different from advertising. When you engage in advertising, your company pays for the space and time of an advertisement (or commercial, which is an insert appearing on radio, television, or the Internet).

On the other hand, when a business or PR firm issues a news release (also referred to as a press release or media release), any editorial coverage acquired through public relations is not paid for by the business or the PR firm. If your story is considered newsworthy, the media will pick it up and publish it.

Public relations is "earned media:" coverage received in magazines, newspapers, radio, or television that happens without spending any money. That's my favorite part, and it's easier to get free attention than you think. It's really a matter of knowing what to do.

For starters, you have to have something to offer. What is happening in your business that is newsworthy? Media publications are in the business of providing either valuable or entertaining content—and sometimes both—for their readers If you can't spin your product to provide this kind of content, your story is never going to get picked up. This is probably the most fundamental principle in the media industry, yet it is often the most ignored. Instead, business owners focus on their product and why their product should be featured. This leads to rejection after rejection, and in the rare cases when stories do get published (because the writer had nothing else to write about), the story gets ignored.

WHAT INFORMATION IS NEWSWORTHY?

It is important to know what types of stories journalists are interested in, as this can determine whether or not your story gets covered. Below are topics that the media usually will find of interest:

Product launches, the announcement of a store opening, or notice of a new location. Contact the media if you are launching a new brand or service, or opening a new branch, or even having an anniversary celebration.

Human interest story. A newsworthy story may convey a story about a person or persons in an interactive and emotional way. The story usually presents people and their problems in a way that brings about interest or sympathy from the reader. Do you have a human interest story that you could share?

Partnerships. This type of announcement is appealing to the media if it affects other industries or an international company. Even a short term partnership with another person or company that is of interest to the public can be an appealing piece of information.

Industry recognition. If your business wins an award recognized by the industry, this would be of interest to the press.

Now that you know what is deemed newsworthy, let's move on to the basic principles of launching a public relations campaign. I will also cover online tools you can use to distribute your press release. Some of the tools are free, while some cost a little money. It should be noted that by the time you are done reading this chapter (and the Best Practices section in particular), you should have a strongly developed sense of how to run a basic PR campaign for virtually no money. It will require time and effort, but the potential to reach hundreds, thousands, or millions of users is unmatched.

In the Best Practices section, which is probably the most important section of this chapter, the emphasis will be on the best approach for getting your story published. Like the Best Practices I have featured so far, the main focus is on treating other people with respect and providing value. I can't guarantee that following the guidelines provided will get your story in front of millions of viewers for free, but you will have a greater chance than the person who just throws something together without any structure or know-how.

4.2 How to Get the Media's Attention

We all know the stresses that reporters face, so keep in mind some basic guidelines when trying to attract press for your product or service.

For starters, you need to understand that individuals, not all-powerful magazines or newspapers, write stories. There is no writer named New York Times or Inc. These are simply names of publications. However, it's the people who produce content for these publications that make the publications the mega-brands they are. The point here is that you should be pitching individual reporters and not media outlets in-and-of themselves.

Fig. 4.1 Public relations helps to build relationships with prospects, clients, and communities.

How does one go about doing this? Build a relationship with reporters. Building authentic relationships with potential business partners is one of the most basic tenets of business, yet it has been forgotten in the modern age of instant gratification and modern technology. To give you an example of how much a difference building a relationship can mean, take a look at the two emails below:

#1—Dear Reporter,

I have a story I think your publication will be very interested in. Just this last week we developed a software prototype that is going to change social media marketing forever. I know you don't know me, but this software is truly amazing; you have to check it out.

#2—Dear Samantha,

How are you? I saw your piece on XYZ that came out in ABC magazine last week and loved it. Today I wanted to let you know about something our company is doing that I believe your readers would be highly interested in. I know your publication focuses on email marketing, and we just finished coding a product that tracks email content when it is shared across social networks...

Do you see the difference between these two emails? If you don't, reread them until you do. Which one would you send if you had a basic relationship with the reporter? I am in no way implying that you need to become best friends with the reporters you want to publish your stories; that would take way too much time. However, developing a relationship with them so that they know who you are can mean the difference between whether they read your email and give it consideration, or instantly hit Delete. And if you have done your homework and know for a fact that your piece offers value (or entertainment) to their readers, there is no reason they shouldn't publish it.

So how do you develop a relationship with a reporter? Easy—become genuinely involved in their work life. Follow them on Twitter and Facebook, Retweet their content (periodically), and email them stories that are relevant to their work and that might provide them with ideas for future stories.

And if you really want to build a relationship, provide them with cutting-edge information on your industry. If you provide a reporter with information that no one else (or few others) have, they will love you for it. And if you give them the first scoop on a big development in your industry, you will have a new best friend.

It should be noted that developing these relationships need not take a long time. You can easily create a (private) Twitter list of the reporters you want to work with. From there, go through and Retweet the content you find interesting. Take a few minutes to comment on their blogs or the stories they have published online. Share their stories on Facebook. If you do this often enough they will notice you, guaranteed. Just don't try to make it happen too fast. It will be very obvious if you pop out of nowhere and begin sharing and Retweeting every piece of content they post and commenting on online articles they wrote six months ago. In short, use common sense and approach the process from a genuine place.

No matter how great a relationship you have with a reporter, if your content does not fit the angle or target audience of their publication, the reporter will not be able to cover your story (no matter how much they love you). How do you address this? Once again, you just have to do a little homework.

Before establishing relationships with reporters, make sure that the publications they work for are the type your target audience consumes. As an example, building a relationship with a reporter who writes for AARP (American Association of Retired People) magazine is probably not a good idea if your target audience is made up of teenagers. This would seem like common sense, but many marketers make these kinds of mistakes.

Before you write your first press release or contact your first journalist, do an in-depth analysis of the publications where you want your stories to be run. Who is their target market? Who reads their content? What is the angle of their magazine? Are they cutting-edge or do they prefer traditional content? Are they liberal or conservative? Do they give preference to green companies?

If you're not sure where to start, read the stories that are getting press in your target publications. Analyze the angle the writers are using, how technical their articles are, how much of the article is the writer's opinion, and how much content is coming from the company the story is about, etc. There is no better way to get a feel for the type of story a publication would accept than by analyzing the stories they already run.

By analyzing publications, you can weed out those whose target audiences or angle least matches up with the story you want to run. Further, analyzing publications ensures that the contacts you establish will be of use to you. You may not be published the first time you make a request, but at least you will know your relationship-building efforts have not been wasted.

And if your reporter-friend doesn't accept your story, don't throw the relationship away because it did not work out the first time. The story may have been rejected because the approach you took wasn't a proper fit for the publication. This does not mean you have to abandon the story. It simply means you need to tweak it a little bit so that it better fits the publication's angle and audience.

4.3 How to Write a Press Release

> A *press release*, sometimes referred to as a media release or news release, is a printed or electronic document issued by entrepreneurs, non-profits, or businesses who want to communicate news to editors, journalists, industry writers, or other media groups.

If journalists feel the content in your press release is considered newsworthy, they will write a story for their publication.

The press release is one of the most important tools an entrepreneur or small business can have in a public relations program. It can quickly communicate to a journalist who you are, what your business is about, and why their readers would be interested.

The news release contains important facts, quotes from key people, dates that the news happened (or will happen), and contacts for additional information. Your news release must be clear and concise. It normally runs no longer than two pages.

Practice the Five Ws

Editors know best what their readers are interested in. They follow the five Ws tradition of reporting: who, what, where, when and why (and sometimes how). When drafting your news release pitch, make a point to answer the five Ws. Use the five Ws as a means of getting the attention of the editors you are pitching to.

When you tell your story, make the news interesting and relevant to the publication's audience. I cannot stress that enough. Your release must be timely and newsworthy. Understanding the five Ws (plus "how") will help you to craft your story. The who, what, where, when, why and how are the six vital ingredients of all press releases.

The **"what"** is the subject of your release— a product launch, new management appointment, or an interesting event. It is the subject or the "hook" that grabs attention.

The **"who"** usually consists of your company, spokespersons, or other authorities quoted in your news release. It mentions all the people involved. The "who" could also be the person(s) in the press release who is providing the quote or statement.

The **"where"** is the location that the newsworthy event has taken place or will take place.

The **"when"** is the date and/or time that the specific event took place or will take place. "When" is a key element. Your press release must be timely. Submit it just before the event or immediately after for it to be considered news.

The **"why"** is what makes the story important or newsworthy to the public. This is where you are sharing the reasons that this event will have an impact on the readers.

Fig. 4.2 Inverted Pyramid Journalism

(Source:www.allstream.com/smallbusiness)

With the five Ws covered, the next step is to structure the release so that it gets the media's attention.

THE STRUCTURE OF A PRESS RELEASE

The parts of a press release are the headline, the first paragraph, the middle paragraphs, and the final details.

THE HEADLINE

This is the very first thing that any editor will read. The headline should be one sentence that captures the core announcement and includes a keyword. A weak headline will often result in a release being rejected from the very start. Write a headline that will create an impact, using eye-catching words such as "announces" and "new" if this is true. You don't want to risk losing your credibility if it is not. Your headline must be compelling, as this is the hook that grabs the editor's attention and gets them reading more.

Because the headline is such an important aspect of getting your press release read, I want to spend a few moments on this topic. When it comes to writing headlines, one free tool that I use every time I write a press release headline, subject line. and even book title is a Headline Analyzer. The one I use is the online Headline Analyzer from the Advanced Marketing Institute.

This tool will analyze your headline to determine the Emotional Marketing Value (EMV) score. Your headline will be reviewed and scored based on the total number of EMV words it has in relation to the total number of words it contains. This will determine the EMV score of your headline.

We all know that people react mainly on emotions and logic follows, so reaching your customers in a deep and emotional way is a key to successful copy writing. No doubt about it, your headline is the most important piece of copy you can write. But first you have to connect with the media.

In addition to the EMV score, the analyzer will allow you to find out which emotion your headline will impact customers: Intellectual, Empathetic or Spiritual.

Note: I want to add that the Headline Analyzer can also be used when you are creating the subject headlines for your newsletters, e-flyers (also referred to as an EDM – electronic direct mailer). I even use this tool for reviewing my book titles and subtitles and when deciding on my workshop titles.

WRITING HEADLINES:

- Determine the most significant benefit the reader will derive from this news.

- Strive to state the benefit in seven words or less.

- Ask yourself if your statement is meaningful to someone not involved with the business.

- Use the ideal font type of Times New Roman, size14 pt. The headline should be bold and centered and below the header "FOR IMMEDIATE RELEASE."

- Try to fit the headline on one single line, using eight to ten words.

- Use the active voice and the present tense.

When crafting the headline, strive to achieve the greatest impact using the fewest words. Editors look for information in the headline, so do your best to at least include who, what and why.

See the following example:

SMEs March into the Marketing Bootcamp to learn Social, Video and Mobile Phone Marketing Strategies to Leverage their Business.

SUB-HEADLINES

The purpose of the sub-headline is to expand on the core announcement. The subheadline should be one sentence. Not all press releases have a sub-headline. Take note that some online press release distributors might require a sub-headline, so prepare one prior to logging in. This will save you from rushing and throwing something together just for the sake of getting it done.

WRITING SUB-HEADLINES:

- Use the ideal font type of Times New Roman, size 12 pt. The sub-headline should be bold, italicized (optional), centered, and below the headline.
- Amplify the headline and introduce one additional key point.
- Aim for keeping the sub-headline to one sentence of no more than 14 words.

THE FIRST PARAGRAPH

A large number of press releases are accepted or rejected based on the headline and the first paragraph or two. Editors maintain a busy schedule and sometimes only have time to read the first paragraph—also referred to as the lead paragraph. A press release may be rejected simply because the lead paragraph failed to contain any news.

> The lead paragraph should contain your key message and take only 30 seconds to read aloud. Editors are looking for you to include the five Ws in the first few sentences.

Below is an example from a press release I used for the announcement of a marketing bootcamp for small businesses owners. Can you identify the 5Ws?

Singapore, 16th February, 2014 - Like platoons on a mission, SMEs across multiple industries will have the opportunity to participate in the inaugural **SME Marketing Bootcamp** on **27-28th March, 2014** at the **Amara Singapore Hotel**. Attendees will learn strategies for social networking, video and mobile phone marketing which they can immediately implement to leverage their business. The SME Marketing Bootcamp is a collaboration between **Experiential Hands-on Learning and STJOBS** (a division of Singapore Press Holdings).

Fig. 4.3 Example of first paragraph of a press release using the 5Ws

THE MIDDLE PARAGRAPHS

The next sections of your press release are the middle paragraphs or body text. Limited space in publications and limited time in broadcasting means that only the first paragraph may get covered. Keep the content in the middle paragraphs conversational, using short words and sentences with a paragraph size of about 40 words.

You should have your paragraphs ordered by importance, because editors may scan the release quickly and not get to the end. Rank the most important information and place it in your release accordingly. Usually, sequence indicates importance. Stacking your news in what is referred to as the inverted pyramid can tell editors the relative importance of your information.

THE FINAL DETAILS

Now that all of your content is complete, you need to mark the end of your news release so that the journalist is aware that there is no further information. This can be done in one of three ways: by putting "-30-"or "-end-"or ### at the bottom, centered after the last line of copy.

CONTACT DETAILS

Make it easy for people to reach you for more information or for an interview. Provide as many ways to contact you as possible. Your contact details may go at the top or the bottom of the page. I believe that it makes it easier for the journalist to find the contact information when it is all at the top. The editor may wish to contact you to check certain details for accuracy. List your information stacked as follows:

Contact person: your name
Tel: +(Area or Country code) 1234 5678
Fax: +(Area or Country code) 1234 8765
Email: pr@companyabc.com
URL: http://www.companyabc.com

A word of caution. Refrain from giving out your cell phone number on a media release unless it is the only means of contacting you. If you decide to submit your press release to a news agency, your cell phone gets published for the whole world to see. You will want to avoid receiving unsolicited calls unrelated to your release. I suggest getting a separate number which you can then have forwarded to your main cell phone number.

Here is one other point to consider: your email address. When uploading your release to free and paid distribution sites, create a separate email address. If sending to different publications, create a new company email address for every new publication or distribution service. There are two reasons to do this. First, it allows you to see which emails are coming from what publication and second, again it protects you from unsolicted emails that come from people surfing the net for active email addresses.

I suggest that you not give away your primary email address; rather create something along the lines of media@companyabc.com, prmanager@companyabc.com, or press@companyabc.com.

RELEASE DATE

Once your story is complete, you will want to notify the media that the information is ready for distribution. At the top of your press release you will want to write, "**For Immediate Release**" **or** "**For Release.**" If your release is to go out at a later date, specify the date to be released. Food for thought: you may wish to hold sensitive information until the time is just right for sending it out, as there is no guarantee that the media will hold the news until your preferred release date.

Journalists are bombarded with press releases and stories all the time, so if you get rejected, don't take it personally. As a matter of fact, embrace rejection. In the world of sales, it is said that every "no" gets you closer to a "yes." Getting rejected may not be fun, but if you have built a relationship with the reporter in the right way, he or she is most likely rejecting your story because it doesn't fit the publication. Just as you wouldn't break up with your boyfriend or girlfriend after your very first fight, don't throw the relationship away the first time the reporter says no. Instead, take a closer look at your pitch (story idea) and fix it.

To tweak your story so that it better fits the publication, there are a couple of things to keep in mind. First of all, publications don't care about your product or service. All they care about is providing value or entertainment to their readers. This is the second most important principle in PR, and one that is also ignored 95 percent of the time.

How does this relate to you? Well, when crafting your press release, stop thinking about how great your product or service is and start thinking about how your product or service solves a pain-point for the publication's audience. This is a well-understood principle in marketing that carries over directly to PR.

When you are writing a sales letter, you should not focus on the features of your product. For example, a list of features for a high-speed laptop would include references to having 8 GB of RAM, a solid-state hard drive, and a core i5 processor. Unless you know computer lingo, these terms mean absolutely nothing. Instead, what marketers should focus on are the benefits, not the features. So instead of talking about RAM and processors, the marketer should focus on how having 8 GB of RAM allows your computer to process various tasks as fast as possible, and how solid-state hard drives are four times faster than regular hard drives.

> So, when you are crafting your press release, think about how your product or service benefits the readers of your target publication and write from that angle.

Talk about how your product or service can save users time or money, increase productivity, etc. If possible, quote statistics, facts, and research. But don't go overboard. Unless you are in a highly technical industry, your release should be relatively light-hearted (and if possible, fun). The more casual your industry is, the more light-hearted your release should be.

In the next section, I will discuss ways to distribute your press release online. Consider this section an introduction to distribution, as there are literally hundreds if not thousands of tools you can use to distribute your content online automatically.

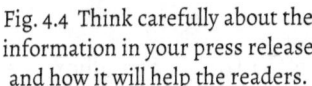
Fig. 4.4 Think carefully about the information in your press release and how it will help the readers.

4.4 HOW TO DISTRIBUTE YOUR PRESS RELEASE ONLINE

Did you know that there are a million and one ways to get press, especially online? Unfortunately, for the most part, the majority of tools are ineffective. As a matter of fact, unless you have earth-shattering news, it is highly unlikely that any automated service is going to get you serious exposure. However, if you have cutting-edge information that is relevant to your industry or target market, using automated tools to get the word out is the easiest and fastest way to get massive exposure.

In general, establishing relationships with reporters is the most effective way to get press while ensuring your message reaches the right audience, but the process of building relationships takes time. If you don't have time to build relationships, or you just stumbled upon some earth-shattering news and don't care what outlets it gets published in as long as the word gets out, then by all means feel free to use automated services.

Some of the services listed below are free and some require a fee. In general, the more you pay, the more exposure you get. However, the more earth-shattering your news is, the less it is going to matter how much exposure you get through an automated tool. Once the story gets picked up and run by a few publications, the word will spread like wildfire.

Free Tools

Distributing your press release online for free is actually rather easy. It is beyond the scope of this book to cover all of the free services, but a quick Google search for "free press release distribution" will get you started. To help you select from the long list that you'll get with a Google search, here are five sites that I have used at some point over the past ten years: PRlog, 24-7Pressrelease, 1888PressRelease, PRBuzz. and PRLeap. .

You'll need to register in advance with theses distributors by giving your name and email details to sign in and submit your release. Once you've uploaded your release, do not be surprised if the site asks you to upgrade to a paid service. You will still have the option to select the free service.

Another means for distributing releases without spending tons of money is Fiverr. Fiverr.com is a website where people offer a variety of services for $5. In the Online Marketing section, you will find individuals offering paid press release distribution for $5, and some of them include paid premium distribution to networks like Google News, SBWire, PRBuzz, and others. The cool thing about using these services is that there is very little downside but potentially huge upside.

Fig. 4.5 Low-cost press release distribution services can be obtained through Fiverr.

Once again, getting access to a network does not mean you will get published. It simply means your release will be available to the network writers. With Google News, things are a little different, as Google News is made up of content from a wide variety of news sites that may or may not be featured on their home page on any one day. In these situations, Comments, Likes, and Retweets play a major factor in getting a story up to the home page. Therefore, you have virtually nothing to lose if you pay for three or four of these gigs (Fiverr jobs) apart from $15-20 dollars. On the flip side, you could get the same level of exposure that one of those $350 packages would have provided for pennies on the dollar—that is, if your content is interesting enough.

Some sites offering free services might ask you if you wish to make a donation. I found that if I was able to give at least $5 or $10, my release was vetted and uploaded faster than when I just clicked the free button.

Another issue to be aware of with free distributors is that it may take up to 24 hours to upload your release. Some sites will have someone to manually review your press release before it is added to their site directory. Make sure you give yourself plenty of time to submit your media release so that it is still timely when it is published.

Yes, you can get free distribution, but paying to distribute it gets it into a much larger network. I will be the first one to use guerrilla marketing tactics, however as you will see there are advantages to using a paid service.

Paid Tools

Although there are strong advantages to opting for a paid service, distributing press releases without knowing how these tools really work is one of the biggest mistakes first-time marketers make. They spend $400 to get their release distributed to the largest newspaper in the United States, only to find out their story didn't get covered—and they just wasted $400. You can imagine how frustrating this is. Be aware that the majority of articles submitted via paid distribution services do not get published. Given this fact, it is extremely important that you think very hard about how valuable your content is before paying hundreds of dollars to distribute it.

Let me be clear: I'm not saying not to use paid services. The key is knowing how these services work and that is what I am going to share with you . When you have a better understanding of what to expect and how to approach paid services, you'll be grinning from ear to ear when you see your results.

In short, the more you pay, the more networks your release will be distributed to. For example, a mid-level package may include exposure to Google News and other major news websites, while a top-level package may include exposure to the New York Times, USA Today, and the like. It should be noted that just because you pay for these packages, it is not guaranteed that your story will be run in the NY Times; it simply means your content will be placed in front of their writers. If, and only if, a writer selects your piece will it be covered in their publication. (Before you submit a release to a paid (or free) service, be sure that your content follows the writing guidelines outlined in this chapter.)

One advantage of a paid service is that you have the ability to upload images, video and your logo. In addition you have the means to track how many person's or companies received your release, what websites have picked up your story for their site, as well as how many media contacts accessed the release. Today many of the press release services include posting to social media sites as well.

When it comes to paid distribution, I encourage you to go this route because of the ability to add images and video. Research shows that images expand your audience up to 180 percent and a custom mix of photos, videos and multimedia content increases it up to 970 percent. To me this is a no brainer as to which way to go.

Be sure that, when you add video to your press release, avoid being a talking head. Include graphics and elements that are engaging to the viewer. Keep it less than 60 seconds if you can.

Once again, getting access to a network does not mean you will get published. It simply means your release will be available to the network writers. With Google News, things are a little different, as Google News is made up of content from a wide variety of news sites that may or may not be featured on their home page on any one day. In these situations, Comments, Likes, and Retweets play a major factor in getting a story up to the home page. Therefore, you have virtually nothing to lose if you pay for three or four of these gigs

(Fiverr jobs) apart from $15-20 dollars. On the flip side, you could get the same level of exposure that one of those $350 packages would have provided for pennies on the dollar—that is, if your content is interesting enough.

And if you are looking for something that allows for a little more control but does not cost hundreds of dollars, there are services that fall into this category. One interesting site to check out is PitchEngine. With plans ranging from $19 to $99 per month, PitchEngine offers content distribution without a high price tag.

Fig. 4.6 Press release distribution using PitchEngine focuses on the social media audience.

PitchEngine's services are more focused on social media distribution than on typical press release outlets. This could be of great value for businesses whose operations are consumer-oriented. If your content is of significant value to consumers, they will be just as likely to share your content on social networks as the publications will be to share it with their audiences. PitchEngine also allows you to include up to three images and to embed video into the release. How cool is that!

Configuring a campaign with PitchEngine will take more time than copying and pasting a release into a service like PRWeb and hitting Send, but it will also give you significantly more control, as well as insight into how your content is being shared. One of the main benefits of using PitchEngine is that they offer extensive tracking and analytics, especially in the social media space.

Describing PitchEngine's services in more detail is beyond the scope of this book and the platform continues to evolve.

Whether you submit your release with a free or fee-based distribution service, post the release to your own website, This can be listed within the "About Your Company" area of your website or under your Press page. In addition, send it out to your clients and post on social media.

4.5 Media Monitoring and Evaluation

What is media monitoring and evaluation?

Once you begin to obtain printed articles or stories in newspapers and magazines about your company it is important to keep track of this information, yet this record-keeping can be a very time consuming process.

> Media monitoring is the activity of monitoring (or keeping watch) on the print, online, and broadcast media coverage that you receive.

There are services that get paid to read, research, and keep track of every media mention of your business, and to make clippings of each article.

Having articles or stories written about your company helps to build credibility about your product or service. A story in the paper is a like an unspoken third party endorsement for your business, as this is not paid advertising, but rather earned advertising.

Printed articles should be collected and kept in good condition so that quality reprints can be made. These reprints will become part of your press kit so that potential customers can see that you have earned media attention.

Articles can also be kept and put up on the media page of your website. Check with your local newspaper agencies before posting, as some publishers may not allow copies of articles to be featured on sites other than their own.

If you've received coverage from a magazine, put a high resolution copy of the magazine cover with a click through to the article as it appears in the magazine. Include the publication name and date below the magazine cover image.

How to monitor media

Start a clip book.

A clip book is a great way to capture and monitor the results of your PR efforts. Putting together a clip book is a tedious process, but it demonstrates your ability as a publicist and shows that you do have a relationship with the media.

Use online tools

To monitor information about your company on the web, news, forums, blogs or on videos, use tools like Google Alerts. Sign up for a free account and then put in the phrases that you want to receive an alert about. The alerts notify you anytime your name or company name appears in news online.

4.6 Best Practices for Dealing with the Media

Up to this point, the aim of this section was to hammer home the importance of approaching PR from a certain point of view. The angle I recommend you take when beginning a PR campaign is this: ask yourself, "How can I provide value to the readers of this publication, and what can I do to increase the likelihood of getting my story published?"

In terms of providing value, follow the guidelines listed in this chapter. Focus on how your product or service benefits the publication's audience instead of why readers should buy your product or service. In terms of how you can increase your chances of getting published, establish real relationships with reporters and journalists so they don't think you are trying to sell them something when you propose a story. In short, approach PR with a genuine interest in helping other people and you will be significantly more successful than 95 percent of the marketers out there.

As for specifics, there are some Do's and Don'ts in this industry. Once again, most of them come down to respect, but they are highlighted here for you just the same.

As for things you should do, be persistent. Treat PR like sales. Know that you are going to get rejected, and pick yourself up every time. Second, be flexible. If your story doesn't get flat-out rejected, you may be approaching it from the wrong angle. Third, be respectful. Understand that reporters have deadlines. Just because you got a reporter to accept your story does not mean your work is done. Make sure the reporter has everything he or she needs to run a great piece, and on time. Taking care of these details not only ensures that you get published; it sets up a positive relationship for the future.

As for things you should not do—don't be a pest. Sending three and four emails to confirm that a reporter received your release is likely to annoy the reporter, and is not going to increase your odds of getting published. Second, don't overstep your boundaries. There is no reason for you to contact a head editor unless you know him or her directly. If your story is good enough, trust that the reporter will either let the editor know, or that the editor will contact you when the reporter turns it in and he or she realizes how great a story it is.

In short, treat people with respect and provide value, and you will be well on your way to running a successful PR campaign.

In the next chapter, I will discuss video marketing, one of the most powerful things you can do to market your business and yet for many, just the idea of video marketing sends a chill down people's spine.

4.7 TAKE ACTION EXERCISE

1. Know your target media. Make sure you are familiar and up-to-date with the types of magazines and newspapers that you are targeting. Do they match the readers that you are aiming to reach? Read current issues, and read a few back issues as well so you get a feel for the style and tone of the magazine.

2. Build a press contact list. You can build your lists through contacts at trade shows or by politely reaching out to key journalists and reviewers, introducing yourself as a prospective resource, and asking nothing more than to keep your information handy and allow you to send them your news.

3. Practice writing eye-catchy headlines that grab attention. Use the Headline Analyzer to see what EMV score you get and keep tweaking until you at least hit a 40 EMV score or above.

4. Develop a pitch. Write a press release or pitch, making sure you keep your target publications' audience and goals in mind.

5. Provide a picture whenever possible. We've all heard the saying that a picture is worth a thousand words. A great photo potentially could make the difference in whether your story gets covered in a local newspaper. Make sure that the image provided is of high resolution print quality.

6. Distribute your press release. Get your newsworthy story in front of potential outlets either directly, or through distribution services. Don't forget to add it to your website too.

Chapter 5

Video Marketing

5.1 INTRODUCTION

To give you an idea of how popular online video has become, YouTube's VP of Global Content recently said that online video will soon account for 90 percent of online traffic. Ninety percent! If that statistic alone doesn't have you considering video as a marketing channel, you need to get with the times.

Aside from the explosive growth that online video has experienced over the past few years, numerous studies show the following: video is preferred to text; users who watch video are more likely to convert into buyers; executives are more likely to navigate to a vendor's page after viewing video; and users who view videos are more likely to stick around on your site for longer. Think of it this way: if a picture is worth a thousand words, then a video must be worth a million. What better way for you to engage with prospects and customers than video?

Up until recently there have been limitations to using video as a marketing channel. Video production has a reputation for being expensive, and finding quality producers means paying top dollar. On top of this, having the video edited to professional standards also costs money.

> Today, advances in technology have allowed virtually anyone with a smartphone and a modern computer to become an amateur video producer.

Okay, stop right there. I can already hear the conversation in your head. I can already hear you saying, "That's great that it's easy to record and edit a video today, but there's no way I'm going to get in front of the camera to record a promotional video."

I must admit, that was me too. Then my husband reminded me that as a professional speaker I get in front of large audiences all the time, so what's the big deal about getting in front of a smart phone and recording a video? He was right. I just had to jump in and do it. The best part is if you don't like the bad takes, you can delete them and start all over.

I will admit, getting in front of the camera is not for everyone, but you need not worry. Instead of speaking into the camera, you can use video clips (or video-like image compilations) to tell the story of your company. You can record your own voice speaking over the video, or hire a freelancer to make a professional voiceover recording.

Now that you're relieved that you don't have to be in front of the camera, or use your own voice for the audio, I want to really impress upon you why it's so important to create videos for your business.

5.2 Why Video is Important for Small Businesses

As indicated above.

> Online video has become the digital media that consumers prefer. This does not mean that websites, blogs, or podcasts are dead. It does, however, mean that you need to rethink where you are focusing your online marketing budget.

The truth is that video is not going away anytime soon. This means that if you have a website and sell a product or service, you most likely need to have a video presence.

Fig. 5.1 Video has become the digital media that consumers prefer. Video ads are easy for small businesses to implement.

> Aside from the abundant statistics that show online video engagement is increasing, video has proven time and time again to increase conversions. (A conversion means that the user goes beyond simply viewing the website to purchasing a product, signing up for a newsletter, etc.)

Which means that if you are in the business of making sales online, you need to test your landing pages (by using some that include video and some that do not). Research shows that women make a decision to stay on a website within five seconds, while men are a bit more generous with their time, staying at least ten seconds. A video on the home page and videos on your other pages will keep people on your site longer.

And while decent quality video production may have cost thousands of dollars in the past, expense is no longer an issue. With a variety of companies introducing stands and hand-held stabilizers for smartphones, virtually anyone with a smartphone can become a video producer. And if you are thinking to yourself, "Well the videos on those phones can't be very good," think again. Starting with the 4, Apple made a serious effort to improve the quality of the camera embedded in iPhones, and with each new version they release, the camera only gets better. The same goes for the Android phones; the Samsung Galaxy S4 has one of the best cameras today. Cameras are only getting better as the smartphones evolve.

This in no way implies that you have to use a smartphone to shoot your video. But if money is an issue, do not exclude video from your campaign because you cannot afford expensive equipment. A fun video shot from a smartphone may come off as more authentic than a professionally produced video. But be sure to keep it classy and professional; just because you can make a smartphone video in five minutes does not mean it is a high quality video.

Think about the format that you currently use to distribute content to your audience. Is your content easy to consume? Today, many things quickly distract people, and attention spans are becoming ever shorter. By adding video to your site, you can keep prospects and customers focused, and help them enjoy consuming your content.

Video content is effective because it increases engagement with your audience in several ways. Videos are visually appealing and the majority of the people that you share your message with enjoy visual content. Think about these YouTube statistics:

- More than 1 billion unique users visit each month.

- Over 6 billion hours of video are watched each month.

- 100 hours of video are uploaded every minute.

Hosting videos on your website and YouTube also does wonders for your SEO. As a small business owner, YouTube is your new best friend, and let me tell you why. In 2006, Google purchased YouTube for $1.65 billion dollars. This was well before the video sharing site was anything like it is today.

As Forrester Research reports, a video properly submitted (title, tags, and description) is 50 times more likely to hit the front page of Google when compared to standard SEO techniques. "How is that," you ask? Well, since Google owns the YouTube brand, Google would prefer to promote their own brand first over other web pages.

In addition, a thumbnail image of the video shows up in the search listing. A thumbnail image is 22 times more likely to be clicked on than the other listings, even if the placement is not in the top three. Again this is based on a properly optimized video, the details of which I will go into in greater detail later in this chapter.

In addition to helping your website rank high in search results and increasing end user "hang time" on your website, video provides a vehicle for educational content marketing. By creating valuable videos and sharing them on YouTube and your website, you cultivate trust with your audience and position yourself as an expert in your field.

Share your videos on platforms like YouTube and WebTV. While YouTube videos should ideally be 1.5 minutes or less, a WebTV series gives you the opportunity to educate your community with 7- to 10-minute videos. This platform is perfect for creating educational, DIY videos for your customers. For example, a florist might create a series of 7- to 9-minute videos on how to create floral arrangements for the different holidays, for dinner parties, or for bridal bouquets, while a property agent could create a video series about home inspections or selling tips. Consider what you can share with your market that would be of interest and where you can educate people who come to your site. Remember, this is not about selling, just entertaining or educating.

It's clear that you need to be creating and sharing videos with your audience, but how, exactly, do you begin?

5.3 WHAT TYPES OF VIDEOS CAN YOU CREATE FOR YOUR BUSINESS?

As a business owner, you have much to discuss. In fact, you have been speaking to your audience in some form since you started your business. he content that you are capable of sharing can be endless. Here are a few types of videos that will help you to get your message out in a big way.

Introductory

An introductory video gives you an opportunity to share information about your product or service. This content gives your audience a lot of value. Remember, attention spans are getting shorter. Visually rich information is easy and fun to consume. Introduce your products and services in a way that appeals to your audience.

Fig. 5.2 Tell a story bigger than your brand.

Tell your Story

Think about what inspires you to offer your service or product to others. It doesn't matter what type of business you are in; there is a backstory that is involved. When your audience understands what drives you to create content, products, and/or services for them, you build trust and credibility. When you share this information in a video you will increase your connection with the people that you want to serve.

Educational

You can enhance your expert status by being an educator in your field. Even though you are in business to generate revenue, you do not always have to promote yourself. What are some of the topics that interest the people in your audience? Be the resource that provides valuable education. Even if you do not create the educational material yourself, the people who view you as a resource will appreciate your willingness to serve them with new and helpful information.

Without a doubt, you want your business to be found online. When you are discovered online, you have the ability to create a strong connection with the people that you want to serve. Your business was created to educate, to inspire, and to serve others. If you implement video into your business strategy, it will be easier and more enjoyable for people to find and consume the important content that you want to share.

5.4. Methods and Tools for Creating Videos

Screen Capture Videos

If you're camera-shy, you can still create engaging videos using screencasting software. What does screencasting software do? You may be familiar with screen shots (screen captures)—pictures of what is on your computer screen. Screencasting is a way to create videos of your screen as you move within a screen or navigate from screen to screen. (Screencasting is often used to demonstrate how a new version of software, such as Excel, for example, works.) For your purposes, you might want to create a PowerPoint presentation describing your product or service. You can then play the PowerPoint on your computer and record and edit it with screencasting software. The result is a video file that you can embed on your website (by first uploading to a hosting service such as YouTube or Vimeo). To see the content of your presentation, users don't have to open PowerPoint; they simply click to watch the video.

Most screencasting software allows you to add audio if you wish. CamStudio, Active Presenter, Jing Project, and Screencast-O-Matic are among the most reliable systems. They capture all screen and audio activity on your computer and create industry-standard AVI

(Audio Video Interleaved or Interleave) files.

CamStudio is an open source (free) program that is available only for Windows (though Mac users can view the videos made with CamStudio). With CamStudio, you can record in AVI format and if you wish, then convert to Flash (SWF files). Flash files take up more room than AVI files, but most people have Adobe Flash. Player installed on their computers so Flash files are easily viewed.

Using ActivePresenter, .you can make your video and easily publish to the web, desktops, or mobile devices without additional editing.

With JingProject you are able to capture an image of what you see on your computer screen and modify it. Simply select any screen or region of a screen that you want to capture, save to your desktop, then draw on it or add a message. You can then upload your media to a free hosting account. You will be given a small URL that you can share with whomever you want. Works with Macs and PCs.

Screencast-o-Matic is a Java-based screencasting tool that requires no downloads and will allow you to automatically upload to hosting. It works well with Macs and PCs.

Another alternative to speaking on camera is to use screenshots, video clips, and image compilations to tell the story of your company. Record your own voice speaking over the video, or hire a freelancer to make a professional voiceover recording.

The above four programs are free. Yes, there are paid programs out there and some free services offer an upgrade to a paid service. My focus with this book is to show you where you can find quality products and services without spending a lot of money. No money is even better, especially when you are just getting started. If you wish to source paid screencasting software, simply contact our friend Google.

Mobile Phone Videos

If you prefer to be in front of the camera, then a talking head video is for you. Shoot a 1- to 2-minute video using your smartphone. Shooting videos in good light is always a plus, yet videos don't have to be professionally lit and shot to engage your audience. In fact, some research shows that homemade videos generate conversions even better than professional videos.

You can also use apps to edit right from your phone and upload directly to YouTube. Most are paid apps ranging from $0.99 to $4.99. Two such apps are MoviePro and SuperImpose Studio. People tend to be more forgiving of the picture quality; however you should strive to have good sound quality. When it comes to making videos using your phone, there are a few small pieces of equipment that will make the job easier.

Fig 5.3 Using your smart phone makes it possible to record anytime, anywhere.

Creating great audio is very important, so one of the best things to do is to invest in a small clip-on microphone. The microphone comes with a cable; one end attaches to your smart phone and the other to your clothes. The one that I use is Audio Technica ATR 3350IS Omni Lavalier Microphone for Smartphones.

Fig. 5.4 Enhance the sound quality of your video with a clip-on microphone.

A tripod also comes in handy. A great one is the JOBY Gorillapod Flexible Tripod. It is small, but it has legs that wrap around just about everything. The last thing you will need is a clip to attach your smartphone to the tripod. I use the **Joby JM1-01WW Grip Tight Mount**. It's foldable and super compact, and easily attaches to your tripod via a ¼-20" screw.

Begin with these three small pieces of equipment and start experimenting with creating your own videos.

Fig 5.5 JOBY Gorillapod Flexible Tripod. A small flexible tripod will help you to stabilize the camera on a desktop or even on a streetlamp or tree.

Studio Videos

The third way to produce a video is with a studio video. This choice tends to be for businesses with sufficient budgets, which allows the option of going into a studio to record.

Before you leap into studio recordings, determine what your objective is for your video. Are you a creating a video about your product, a signature story video, or a WebTV series? Next, spend time interviewing different video production companies to learn which one can best meet your needs.

5.5 Suggested Lengths for Videos

While there is no perfect length for any video, there are guidelines you can follow to ensure your customers get the right amount of information without either leaving too soon or dying of boredom while they wait for something interesting to show up. There are a few different categories for videos, and the category will determine how long it should be.

> If your video is being used primarily for sales purposes, it should be pretty short. Statistics show that every thirty seconds, a substantial percentage of visitors stop watching a video.

This means that the more you can get across in thirty seconds, the better. Unless you are doing a product demonstration or providing detailed information, try and keep your videos under sixty seconds.

If in fact you are providing detailed information or doing a product demonstration, feel free to make your video as long as it needs to be *without going overboard or boring your viewers*. This is crucial. Your product video is like a sales letter. In general there are two forms of sales letters—short form and long form. Thirty to sixty seconds of your most powerful, enthusiastic, engaging content is like a short-form sales letter. If you have already screened visitors and they have a good idea of what your product or service is about, feel free to make your video a little longer.

If your visitors know a little bit about your product or service but do not know everything, it is best to use long-form video. Nobody who clicks on an ad wants to watch a ten-minute video about your product or service. However, if someone has navigated to your site after reading a post on your blog or has arrived at your site through word-of-mouth, showing them a video that enthusiastically describes what your company does will be much more effective than putting a 5,000-word sales letter in front of them.

Seven to ten minutes is most likely the cut-off point for long-form videos. Twenty and thirty minute videos are fine for instructional or educational purposes, but if you cannot convince someone to buy in the first seven to nine minutes of your video, it is highly unlikely they are going to buy. Think about it: if a 5,000-word sales letter cannot convince you to buy, is a 25,000-word letter going to make a difference? Probably not.

This, in turn, brings us to the importance of editing and editing equipment.

5.6 VIDEO EQUIPMENT AND VIDEO EDITING SOFTWARE

When it comes to video equipment, you have hundreds if not thousands of choices. To help you make a selection, here are some very general guidelines, along with a recommendation that you do further investigation online.

For the most part, you want to use something more powerful than a point-and-shoot camera. Point-and-shoot cameras are the small ones that fit in your hand and do not have a very large body. The body is what allows the camera to take higher quality shots, as it houses larger and more powerful lenses, software applications, and more. Let me clarify—you do not need to go out and buy a DSLR (digital single-lens reflex) camera just because it has a large body.

Some of the hybrid cameras are point-and-shoot but have larger bodies that contain a single or multi-flex lens. These hybrids shoot higher quality pictures than point-and-shoots without the expensive price tag of the DSLRs. If you are a beginner and on a tight budget, but want to use something a little more professional than a smartphone, buying one of these hybrids will be your best bet (the Nikon Coolpix L810 is a good buy).

From there, the sky is the limit. The more you spend, the higher quality camera (and therefore video) you are going to get. It should be noted that the cameras mentioned above are not even dedicated video cameras; yet they are still cameras that are capable of producing high-quality video. As technology blurs the lines and combines more features into each model, dedicated video cameras are becoming less popular (except at the highest levels). So you do not necessarily need to invest in a video camera, as almost any still camera is going to offer much more functionality over time (as in the ability to shoot video instead of just photos).

Before I move on, I want to point out that you do not have to buy a camera to produce videos. There are companies you can hire to shoot videos for you on any budget. If your budget is miniscule, it is highly likely that you can find someone on Fiverr to shoot a video talking about your business or demonstrating your product through screen shots. If you have a little more money to spend, some local producers advertising on Craigslist can probably get the job done for a few hundred dollars. And if you have an even larger budget, professional videographers will definitely be able to deliver what you need. Just keep your potential ROI in mind before dropping a significant amount of money.

When it comes to editing programs, virtually every modern computer (on Windows or Mac OSX at least) includes video editing software. While the software may vary depending on the age of your computer, most Windows computers come with Windows Live Movie Maker, while modern Macs come with Apple iMovie. If you are a beginner and do not plan on investing serious money into video over the long run, I recommend you stick with these programs. They may not be the best, and getting accustomed to them may take some time, but the amount of money you will save by not upgrading to professional video editing software is substantial.

If you plan on doing video long-term or you know what you're doing, there are a wide variety of video editing software applications you can use. Some of the most popular are: Adobe Premier Pro

(Windows and Mac OSX), Final Cut Pro (Mac OSX), and Media Composer (Windows and Mac). Which program is best suited for your needs will depend on the system you are using, your budget, and the individual features of each program. It is best that you read consumer reviews and do your homework before investing in expensive software. Anyone who is fully committed to doing video would most likely benefit from investing in one of the more advanced editing programs.

5.7 Optimizing and Uploading Videos

Luckily for us, technology makes putting videos online extremely easy. While there are a multitude of video outlets available online, the two I am going to concentrate on are YouTube and Vimeo. YouTube is by far the largest video site, and includes videos on just about any subject. Vimeo is highly geared towards professionals, business, tech, and other high profit, high impact industries.

Before we get into the ins and outs of how to upload a video, I want to first go over the importance of having your video properly optimized so that search engines can find it. Getting your settings right before you make your video public will help you to be easily found within the platform.

YouTube

I see far too many companies creating videos that are uploaded to YouTube, but will never be found. These videos are titled with the name of the employee who made the video. If no one knows your employee or has a clue about the benefits of the video, only individuals who work for the company will know that the video exists. Or people forget to put in a description and simply hit the upload button. The entire effort ends up being a wasted opportunity because the video is now lost in cyberspace with no way for the average viewer to learn more about your products or services.

A properly optimized video is more likely to get you on page one of Google for the keywords your prospects are likely to enter. So let's get you started on the right track.

Steps for Optimizing your Video

1. The first step for optimizing your video is choosing a good title. If you are trying to optimize your video for search engines, it's best to make the title the keyword. Your title is also the first thing viewers are going to notice about your video. A catchy title is going to attract a much higher number of viewers than a random keyword. Choose wisely, as there are consequences for your choice.

Start with a benefits driven title. Include keywords that speak to the benefits that your video offers.

Here's an example. Let's look at the subject: presentation skills for someone looking to improve their presentation. If you go to YouTube and type in "presentation skills," you will get 1,880,000 results. If you add one word, "tips," so that your search reads "presentation skills tips," you're down to 336,000 video results. Notice how the lower number results from a benefits driven topic, so be sure that you title includes words along those lines.

If you type in "how to present a good presentation" the results bring in 142,000 videos. Therefore, the more specific you can be in your title, the better. People go to YouTube to learn how to do things, so when at all possible, craft your title in a way that matches how people search.

I also recommend that you review section 4.4 on Emotional Marketing Value so that you can choose words for your title that will engage your reader on an emotional level—the most powerful way to get people involved in your subject.

2. The video's description and tags are also very important for search engine rankings and user interaction. As you did (or will do) for your website's meta-description, choose important keywords in the description of your video (without going overboard). Add a brief two to three sentence description about what the video is all about. Again, take advantage of the tools for Emotional Marketing Value explained in section 4.4.

My guess is that people don't write a description because they think that viewers will go ahead and watch the entire video to learn about the topic. Not true. If you don't write a description, you are missing out on a very key optimization component.

You recall I mentioned earlier that Google owns YouTube. As Google crawls the web, the video description gives Google something to read and index within the search engine itself. Without a description, you're making it harder for Google to know what you're all about. This step is KEY so don't skip it.

When writing the description, start by writing out your website or blog URL, using this format: http://yourwebsite.com. Before anyone actually clicks on your video, the URL will show up in the search information. You want your website URL to show up in the results for everyone to see so that when people click to view your video, your website is only one click away. .

Within the description, also include the name of the person speaking (if applicable) as well as your company name. Then end the description again with your full URL: http://yourwebsite.com

The last step for the description is to look to the right side of the YouTube page and find the YouTube URL. It will start with http;//youtu.be/xyz.com. Copy this URL and put it within the description on the line just below your company URL. When you promote your YouTube URL within the description, you are making Google happy by promoting their brand.

3. Write the descriptive tags (keyword phrases) that indicate what the video is all about. As for the tags, YouTube used to show you what tags other videos were using; this allowed you to copy them and get free placement as a "Recommended Video" alongside other videos with the same tags. YouTube has since hidden the Tags section from public view, so consider using a wide variety of one, two, and three word phrases that describe your video. Limit your tags to around six. If you have too many tags, Google will not have a clear understanding of what your video is about and cannot properly index it.

If you are the person speaking in the video (or another staff member for that matter), then always list the person's name and the company name as two of your tags. For one of your tags, include a nonsense or "fake" keyword (like your own name spelled backwards) in every upload, and that custom keyword will then link all of your videos. This means all of your YouTube videos will show up together as related videos.

YouTube makes it very easy to upload videos, but uploading is just one part of the process. While the upload is taking place, there are a couple of settings you need to fill in.

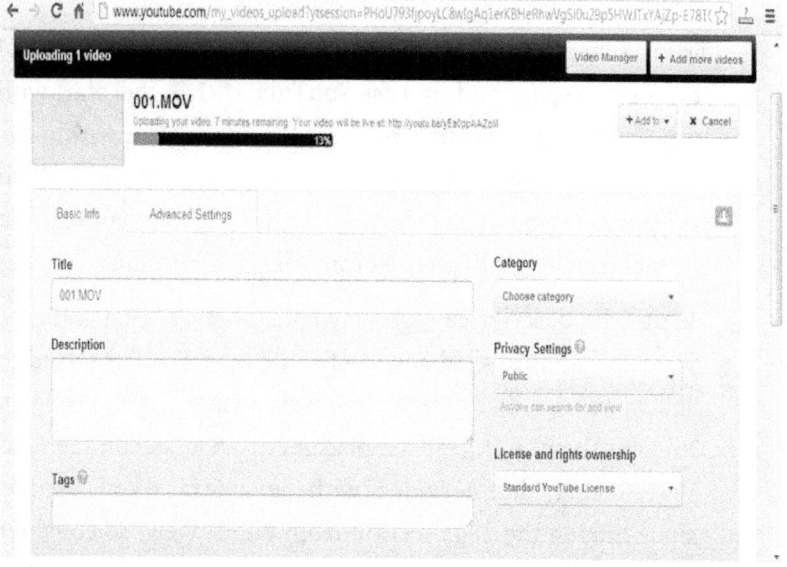

Fig 5.6 Prepare your title, description, and metatags to fully optimize your video.

To upload your video to YouTube, you must first set up an account (or log in using your existing account). Then, click on the Upload link on the top navigation area. You will be taken to a page where you can select the video you would like to upload—or shoot a video using your computer's webcam. From there, simply select the video you would like to upload and begin the process (see Fig. 5.5) as previously outlined.

Once all your settings are complete, add the video to your own website or blog by copying and pasting the "embed code" that YouTube provides. Take note that YouTube also provides a "permalink" that you can use to promote your video via a link in your email or newsletter.

> Link your YouTube account to your social media networks with the one-click share option provided. Once your accounts are linked, you can easily share your video on Facebook, Twitter, and any other social media networks you use.

And last but not least, select the category your video falls into.

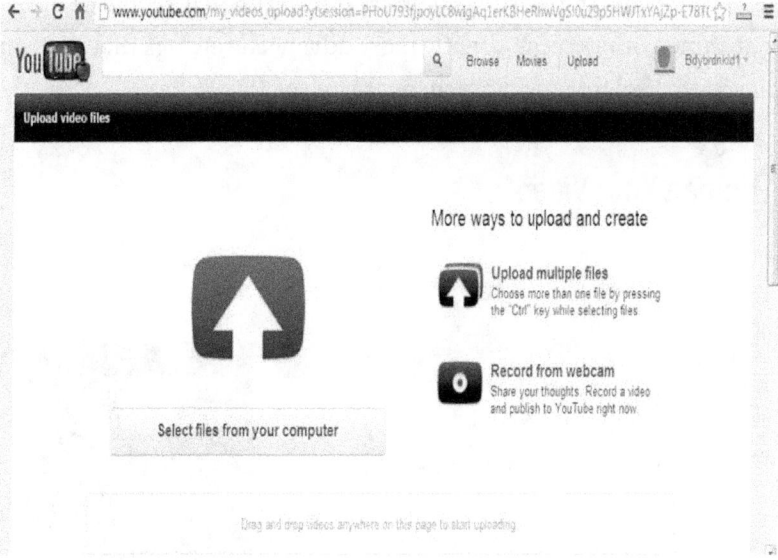

Fig. 5.7 YouTube has the second largest search engine in the world.

Vimeo

Uploading videos to Vimeo is similar to uploading to YouTube. Vimeo asks for your name, email, and creation of a password. On the next page you will be asked to sign up for a paid membership; there are free memberships offered at the bottom of the page in small black text. From there you will arrive at your dashboard. You must confirm that you are the owner of your email account before you can upload. Once this is done, click Upload (see Fig. 5.7).

At this point, you will be taken to a screen where you must agree to Vimeo's guidelines, after which you can select the video you want to upload. Once you have selected your video, you will be taken to a screen where you can adjust various settings, including the description and tags settings (similar to YouTube). It should be noted that Vimeo offers some slightly more advanced settings that you can play with. Feel free to adjust them as you see fit.

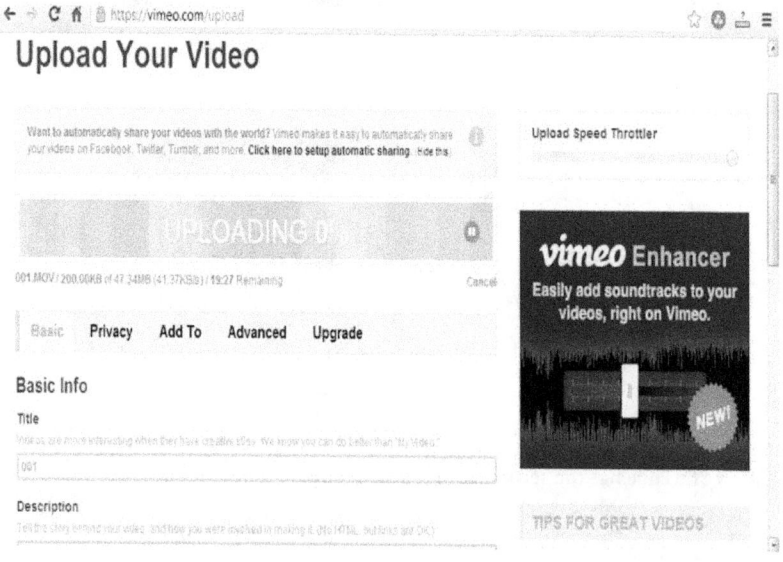

Fig. 5.8 Don't limit yourself to one video directory. Consider using Vimeo in addition to YouTube.

5.6 BEST PRACTICES FOR VIDEO MARKETING

Video today is like the wild, wild west. Aside from following guidelines for copyrighted material and obeying laws regarding sex and minors, there is virtually nothing you cannot do. The good news is you do not have to go to extremes to make an effective video.

Like the best press releases, the best videos are those that offer either serious entertainment or value to the viewers. The more valuable (informative) or entertaining your video is, the more likely it is to succeed. There are countless videos that were shot on a user's webcam that have very high viewership numbers and Thumbs Up counts. (YouTube uses this voting system to determine the popularity of videos.) The more Thumbs Up your video has, the higher YouTube places it in their search results. So the more users Thumbs Up your video, the more viewers you are going to get. Unfortunately this works in the opposite way, too; the more Thumbs Down you get, the lower your video will appear in search results, and the fewer viewers you will get.

This way of ranking videos is actually a highly efficient system, as it tells video producers what is working and what is not. If your video is tied to the right keywords, it is virtually guaranteed to get a couple of thousand views. From there, the main question becomes: did people like the video or not? The voting system will answer this question.

Hint: There is nothing wrong with asking viewers to give your video a Thumbs Up if they liked it. If the content you provided was valuable or entertaining, many of them will. How do you ask? At the end of the video, after thanking your viewers for watching it, request a Thumbs Up.

5.7 TAKE ACTION EXERCISES

1. Assess your needs. Should you invest in recording equipment? Should you hire a professional? Will your available equipment suffice? Decide what your needs are and how your budget can best fill these needs.

2. Familiarize yourself. Get to know the basics of editing software and how to use it to produce quality videos.

3. Identify the needs of your prospects and customers. Their needs will determine what type of video you will make.

4. Create content. Script your video, shoot it (several times, if necessary), and edit it. Review it until you are satisfied with the results. Alternatively, you can outsource the editing process. The goal is to have one or two finished videos.

5. Upload your finished and optimized video content. Get your video in front of an audience. Upload your video onto YouTube, Vimeo, and other appropriate platforms. Invite your viewers to Like and Share and leave comments.

6. Monitor feedback. Ask viewers for feedback. Feedback will allow you to see what works and what doesn't. Use viewer input to focus on positive areas and improve areas that might need some fine-tuning.

Conclusion

In conclusion, it is my hope that you have learned from this guide book and that you are already taking action to accelerate your business. There are hundreds of books and tens of thousands of articles and blog posts written about each topic and sub-topic I have covered. This guide should serve as a launching point for diving more deeply into each of the methods presented.

As you have seen, there is solid reason for investing in each of the marketing channels discussed—Facebook, LinkedIn, Email Marketing, Public Relations, and Video Marketing. While each has advantages and disadvantages, the combination of one or more approaches can be extremely powerful. Be patient; you should not attack all of the channels at once.

Unless you are already an expert in one or more of these areas, do not attempt to manage or create all of these strategies at the same time. As a matter of fact, do not move on to the second strategy until you have successfully implemented the first— and understand it well enough to teach someone else. If you have implemented a strategy and it failed, or if you are not sure enough about the details to teach someone else, you have work to do.

On a different note, I hope you noticed a running theme throughout this guide. Whether you are contacting executives on LinkedIn; emailing journalists in the hope that they pitch your story; creating video content; or emailing a new prospect, there are two things you should keep in mind.

First, treat people with respect. Remember that people do business with people they know, like, and trust. Shady marketing tactics will never get you long-term success; treating people with respect will build partnerships that last a lifetime. Second, provide value. This is the most basic but most overlooked principle in marketing. When you provide enough value to people, they will want to do business with you. Think about it: if someone treats you with respect and provides a solution to a painful problem you are facing, why wouldn't you do business with them?

Unfortunately, this ideal has been lost in the maze of ROI and target markets thinking, but it is probably the most sound business principle that has ever existed. Regardless of what media you are using to reach your audience, keeping these considerations in mind is a guaranteed way to supercharge your marketing efforts.

Here's to your business success!

About the Author

Pamela Wigglesworth is an international speaker, corporate trainer, and Managing Director of Experiential Hands-on Learning, a training and development company. She has resided in Asia for over 24 years, and works with companies across multiple industries to enhance their branding and marketing communications to get big results on a small budget.

Pamela is a Professional member of the Asia Professional Speakers - Singapore (APSS) and served as the 2011-2012 Vice President. She is a member of the Marketing Institute of Singapore and the American Chamber of Commerce in Singapore, and a founding board member of the PrimeTime Business and Professional Women's Association.

She lives in Singapore with her husband John.

www.Facebook.com/Experiential Hands-on Learning

 @ExpPam

 courses@experiential.sg

 www.experiential.sg

 http://www.youtube.com/user/ExperientialSG/

www.ingramcontent.com/pod-product-compliance
Lightning Source LLC
Chambersburg PA
CBHW051811170526
45167CB00005B/1967